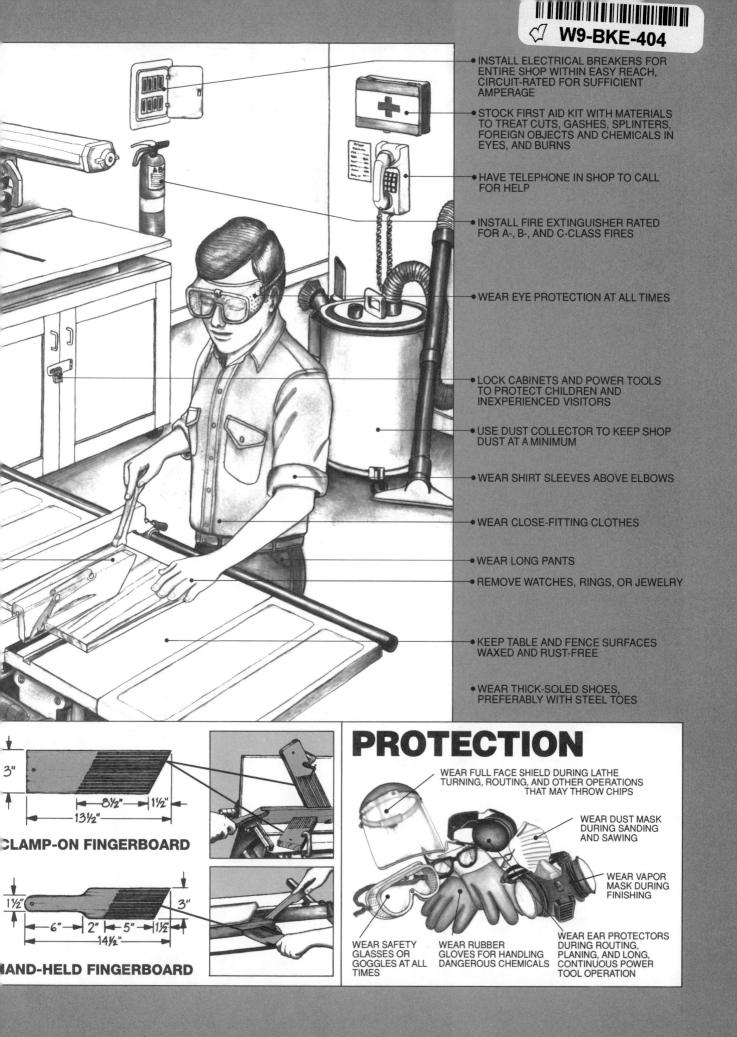

- INSTALL ELECTRICAL BREAKERS FOR ENTIRE SHOP WITHIN EASY REACH, CIRCUIT-RATED FOR SUFFICIENT AMPERAGE
- STOCK FIRST AID KIT WITH MATERIALS TO TREAT CUTS, GASHES, SPLINTERS, FOREIGN OBJECTS AND CHEMICALS IN EYES, AND BURNS
- HAVE TELEPHONE IN SHOP TO CALL FOR HELP
- INSTALL FIRE EXTINGUISHER RATED FOR A-, B-, AND C-CLASS FIRES
- WEAR EYE PROTECTION AT ALL TIMES
- LOCK CABINETS AND POWER TOOLS TO PROTECT CHILDREN AND INEXPERIENCED VISITORS
- USE DUST COLLECTOR TO KEEP SHOP DUST AT A MINIMUM
- WEAR SHIRT SLEEVES ABOVE ELBOWS
- WEAR CLOSE-FITTING CLOTHES
- WEAR LONG PANTS
- REMOVE WATCHES, RINGS, OR JEWELRY
- KEEP TABLE AND FENCE SURFACES WAXED AND RUST-FREE
- WEAR THICK-SOLED SHOES, PREFERABLY WITH STEEL TOES

3"
8½"   1½"
13½"

**CLAMP-ON FINGERBOARD**

1½"
6"   2"   5"   1½"
3"
14½"

**HAND-HELD FINGERBOARD**

# PROTECTION

WEAR FULL FACE SHIELD DURING LATHE TURNING, ROUTING, AND OTHER OPERATIONS THAT MAY THROW CHIPS

WEAR DUST MASK DURING SANDING AND SAWING

WEAR VAPOR MASK DURING FINISHING

WEAR SAFETY GLASSES OR GOGGLES AT ALL TIMES

WEAR RUBBER GLOVES FOR HANDLING DANGEROUS CHEMICALS

WEAR EAR PROTECTORS DURING ROUTING, PLANING, AND LONG, CONTINUOUS POWER TOOL OPERATION

# THE WORKSHOP COMPANION™

# SANDING AND PLANING

## TECHNIQUES FOR BETTER WOODWORKING

by Nick Engler

Rodale Press
Emmaus, Pennsylvania

Printed in the United States of America on acid-free ∞,
recycled ♻ paper

If you have any questions or comments concerning this
book, please write:
    Rodale Press
    Book Readers' Service
    33 East Minor Street
    Emmaus, PA 18098

About the Author: Nick Engler is an experienced woodworker, writer, and teacher. He worked as a luthier for
many years, making traditional American musical instru-
ments before he founded *Hands On!* magazine. Today, he
contributes to several woodworking magazines and teaches
woodworking at the University of Cincinnati. He has written
more than 30 books.

Series Editor: Jeff Day
Editors: Bob Moran
            Roger Yepsen
Copy Editor: Barbara Webb
Graphic Designer: Linda Watts
Illustrator: Mary Jane Favorite
Master Craftsman: Jim McCann
Photographer: Karen Callahan
Cover Photographer: Mitch Mandel
Proofreader: Hue Park
Indexer: Beverly Bremer
Typesetting by Computer Typography, Huber Heights, Ohio
Interior and endpaper illustrations by Mary Jane Favorite
Produced by Bookworks, Inc., West Milton, Ohio

**Library of Congress Cataloging-in-Publication Data**

Engler, Nick.
    Sanding and planing/by Nick Engler.
        p.    cm. — (The workshop companion)
    Includes index.
    ISBN 0–87596–582–2   hardcover
    1. Woodworking tools.   I. Engler, Nick.
        Workshop companion.   II. Title.
    TT186.E52   1993
    684'.08—dc20
                                            93–29729
                                            CIP

4  6  8  10  9  7  5        hardcover

*The author and editors who compiled this
book have tried to make all the contents as
accurate and as correct as possible. Plans,
illustrations, photographs, and text have
all been carefully checked and cross-
checked. However, due to the variability
of local conditions, construction materials,
personal skill, and so on, neither the
author nor Rodale Press assumes any
responsibility for any injuries suffered, or
for damages or other losses incurred that
result from the material presented herein.
All instructions and plans should be carefully studied and clearly understood
before beginning construction.*

Special Thanks to:

Belsaw Co.
Minneapolis, Minnesota

Makita U.S.A., Inc.
La Mirada, California

Performax Products, Inc.
Burnsville, Minnesota

Ryobi America Corp.
Anderson, South Carolina

Vega Enterprises, Inc.
Decatur, Illinois

Wertz Hardware
West Milton, Ohio

Williams & Hussey Machine Co., Inc.
Wilton, New Hampshire

Woodworker's Supply
Albuquerque, New Mexico

# CONTENTS

## TECHNIQUES

# PROJECTS

# TECHNIQUES

# 1

# USING THE JOINTER

For over 4,000 years, from the time that the early Egyptian artisans developed woodworking into a distinct craft, the most laborious and time-consuming part of any woodworking project was surfacing and truing the lumber. A single craftsman often kept several apprentices busy working rough wood down to flat, straight boards with hand planes. It's little wonder that as the Industrial Revolution dawned, surfacing machines were among the first power tools.

In 1793, Sir Samuel Bentham, an English engineer, patented a remarkable collection of woodworking equipment, all designed to be run by the newly invented steam engine. Included in these was "planing machine," a mechanical version of a cooper's jointer. The cooper's jointer, used for truing the edges of barrel staves, was the longest woodworking plane (sometimes over 6 feet in length) and the only one that was held stationary while the wood was passed across it. It was an immensely practical design for a surfacing tool, so much so that the basic form of Bentham's original planing machine has remained in use for 200 years. The name, however, has not survived. Woodworkers preferred to call Bentham's invention for the hand tool it resembled — the jointer.

# CHOOSING A JOINTER

Today, the jointer is an indispensable power tool in any well-equipped cabinet shop. Unless you know the techniques required to true boards with hand planes — and have the time to do it — the jointer is the only tool that will produce perfectly flat surfaces and straight edges.

## HOW A JOINTER WORKS

To use a jointer, you pass a board over two long, narrow tables — an *infeed table* and an *outfeed table*. Between them is a *cutterhead,* which holds two or three *knives.* (The knives are about as long as the tables are wide.) As you feed the stock from the infeed table to the outfeed table, the revolving knives cut the wood straight and flat. The tables and the cutterhead are mounted on the jointer's *base*.

You can adjust the depth of cut by turning the *infeed table adjustment knob*. This raises and lowers the infeed table relative to the cutterhead and the outfeed table. A *depth-of-cut indicator* shows how much the infeed table has moved. Some jointers also have an *outfeed table adjustment knob*. This makes it easier to position the outfeed table and the knives at precisely the same level. If they aren't at the same level, your cut won't be straight. **Note:** Some jointers have adjustment levers rather than knobs.

A *fence* guides the stock as you pass it across the jointer. If you are jointing the face of a board, the fence keeps the board positioned over the cutterhead. If you are jointing an edge, the fence not only positions the board but holds it at the proper angle to the knives. A *fence tilt adjustment* changes the angle of the fence.

A *cutterhead guard* covers the unused portion of the knives when you are surfacing narrow stock or the edge of a board. Some jointers may have a *rabbeting ledge,* which allows you to cut rabbets in the edges of boards. They may also have a *rabbeting notch* in the outfeed table, although this isn't absolutely necessary for cutting rabbets.

The jointer *stand* holds the *motor,* which is connected to the cutterhead with pulleys and a V-belt and is controlled with an *on/off switch*. Because all jointers direct the wood chips down as they cut, the stand also contains a *chip chute* to carry the wood shavings away from the jointer and its motor. (*SEE FIGURE 1-1.*)

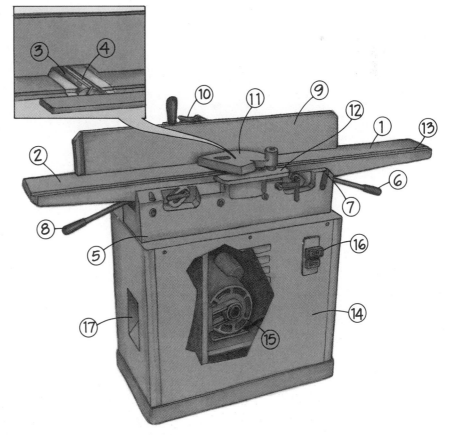

**1-1  A jointer has two long,** narrow tables — an *infeed table* (1) and an *outfeed table* (2). Between them is a *cutterhead* (3) with several *knives* (4). The tables and the cutterhead are mounted in a *base* (5). You can raise and lower the infeed table by turning the *infeed table adjustment knob* (6). A *depth-of-cut indicator* (7) shows how far the table has moved. Some jointers also have an *outfeed table adjustment knob* (8). A *fence* (9) guides the stock over the jointer, and a *fence tilt adjustment* (10) lets you change the angle of the fence. A *cutterhead guard* (11) covers the unused portion of the knives while you cut. There may also be a *rabbeting ledge* (12) and a *rabbeting notch* (13) for rabbeting cuts. The jointer *stand* (14) supports the tool and holds the *motor* (15) and the *on/off switch* (16). A *chip chute* (17) carries the waste away from the machine.

## JOINTER FEATURES

When purchasing a jointer, there are several features to consider:

*Cutterhead size* — The width of the cutterhead and the length of the knives it holds determine the maximum width of the cut. The size you need depends on the type of woodworking you do. If you want a jointer mostly for truing edges and for occasionally flattening the face of a frame member or squaring up leg stock, then a jointer with a 4-inch cutterhead is adequate. For general woodworking, a 6-inch jointer is more useful. Serious craftsmen and owners of small cabinet-making shops prefer 8-inch jointers; larger shops may have 12-inch machines. If you require a jointer with an unusually large capacity, there are even 24- and 36-inch models.

*Table size* — When considering the length of the infeed and outfeed tables, the longer, the better. The long tables provide more support for the stock. Of the two, the length of the outfeed table is more important — it's much easier to get a straight, true surface if the wood is well supported *after* it's cut. (*See Figure 1-2.*)

*Speed and power* — The longer the cutterhead, the more power is required to turn it. An underpowered

jointer may bog down during a wide cut. For 4-inch jointers, a $1/2$-horsepower motor is adequate. Mid-size jointers (6 and 8 inch) should have at least $3/4$-horsepower motors, and if you consistently make wide cuts, they may require up to 2 horsepower. Larger jointers will require proportionately more power. Whatever the power, the motor should turn the cutterhead between 4,000 and 5,000 revolutions per minute (rpm) for a smooth cut. To increase the speed to the desired range, most jointers use a 3,450-rpm motor with a slightly larger pulley on the motor shaft than on the cutterhead shaft.

*Fence mounting* — There are two types of jointer fences, center-mounted and end-mounted. (*See Figure 1-3.*) Center-mounted fences are more stable since they are supported just above the cutterhead — the spot where you're likely to put the most pressure when using the jointer. Additionally, they are safer — the mount covers the unused portion of the knives on the back side of the fence. End-mounted fences may flex if you press too hard when feeding the stock across the machine.

**1-2 A long outfeed table supports** the stock better than a short one and makes it easier to produce straight, true cuts. It also helps when jointing long stock. To joint a long board on a short jointer, you often have to use a roller stand for extra support on the outfeed end. This can be tedious and time-consuming to set up, since the stand must be at *precisely* the same level as the jointer's outfeed table to make accurate cuts.

*Fence tilt* — Almost all jointer fences tilt from 90 degrees (square to the table) to 45 degrees. The most useful fences tilt 45 degrees both right *and* left, adding to the versatility of the machine. When chamfering an edge or truing a bevel, you want to tilt the fence *toward* the table to cradle the stock. This prevents the piece from slipping and makes it easier to joint an accurate angle. However, you must sometimes tilt the fence *away* from the table to accommodate large work-pieces. A fence that tilts in both directions lets you choose the best setup. *(SEE FIGURE 1-4.)*

*Adjustable infeed and outfeed tables* — All jointers have an adjustable *infeed* table. Lower the table to take deeper cuts; raise it for shallower cuts. Some jointers also have an adjustable *outfeed* table, making it much easier to set the knives precisely. To make an accurate cut, all the knives in the cutterhead must be at the same height *and* they must be at the proper height relative to the outfeed table. If the outfeed table is fixed in place, you must set the height of knives as you install them — an exacting and time-consuming process. If the outfeed table is adjustable, you can install the knives so they are all at the same height (a much easier operation), then position the outfeed table relative to them.

**1-3 Center-mounted fences** *(right)* provide better support than the end-mounted variety *(left)*. End-mounted fences are usually attached to the jointer at the infeed end. The standard technique for feeding a board across a jointer is to put most of your pressure over the cutterhead and the outfeed table. Because the mount of an end-mounted jointer fence is so far from the center of pressure, it can be easily flexed by pressing too hard. This, in turn, may interfere with the accuracy of your cuts.

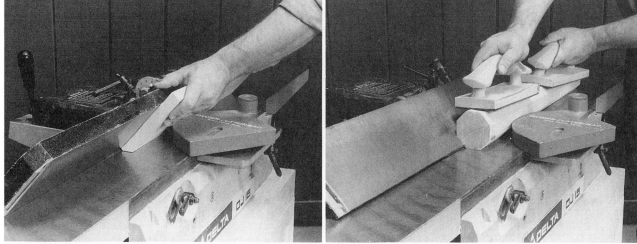

**1-4 The most versatile jointer** fences tilt both left and right. To make accurate bevels and chamfers, tilt the fence to the *left* as you face the infeed table (*toward* the table). The work will be cradled between the fence and the table so it can't slip. To joint large pieces at odd angles, tilt the fence to the *right* (*away* from the table).

Tables are adjusted in various ways. On most jointers, they slide up and down an inclined plane, guided on tracks or dovetail-shaped ways. The tables of newer Delta jointers, however, pivot on parallel hinges. (SEE FIGURE 1-5.) Instead of moving in a straight line, each table moves in an arc. This keeps the tables the same distance away from the cutterhead no matter what the table position. The stock is better supported as it's cut, and the wood shavings are evacuated more efficiently. The hinges are also less likely to become clogged with sawdust than traditional inclined tracks and ways.

*Cutterhead guard* — Although more shop accidents happen on a table saw than with any other power tool, the most serious accidents happen on a jointer. The reason is two-fold. First, a jointer takes a much wider cut than a saw — whereas a saw might remove a few fingers in a careless moment, a jointer will eat your whole hand. Second, once the machine gets hold of you, *it drags you in* like a big meat grinder. Not a pretty thought, is it? For this reason, the cutterhead guard is one of the most important features to consider when selecting a jointer. The guard should be big and painted a bright color, and it must completely cover the unused portion of the knives, no matter what the position of the fence or the width of the workpiece. In addition, the spring must be strong enough to retract the guard quickly once the stock is past the cutterhead.

*Rabbeting ledge* — Some craftsmen consider a jointer with a rabbeting ledge a convenient tool for rabbeting edges. Unfortunately, depending on the dimensions of the rabbet and the workpiece, you may have to remove the guard from the machine. (SEE FIGURE 1-6.) As safety standards have improved over the years, tool manufacturers have wisely made it more difficult to remove cutterhead guards. Some advise against doing it altogether. Consequently, jointers have become less

convenient rabbeting tools than they once were. Furthermore, the jointer knives must be set precisely to cut an accurate rabbet — they must be in the proper relationship to the surface *and* the edge of the outfeed table. There are many other tools that will cut rabbets more safely and more accurately. For these reasons, a rabbeting ledge shouldn't be a big factor in choosing a jointer.

**1-6  A rabbeting ledge allows you** to cut rabbets in the edges of boards. However, you may have to remove the guard to do this, exposing a portion of the cutterhead. If the fence is end-mounted and does not cover the cutterhead on the back side, the *entire* cutterhead may be exposed. For these reasons, *using the jointer as a rabbeting tool may compromise your safety.* Use a table saw, a router, or a dado cutter instead.

**1-5  On most jointers, adjustable** tables move up and down an inclined plane. As you twist the adjusting knobs, threaded bolts pull the tables up or push them down the slope. This movement is guided by interlocking tracks or dovetail ways in the mating surfaces of the tables and the base. An exception to this arrangement is the newer Delta design, with tables that pivot on parallel hinges and that are counterbalanced by tension springs. The motion is controlled by long levers.

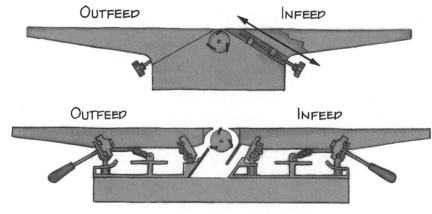

# JOINTER KNOW-HOW

## ALIGNMENT AND ADJUSTMENT

For your jointer to make straight, true cuts, align and adjust it precisely. The tables must be flat and parallel to one another; the knives must be set at the proper height to the outfeed table; the fence must be at the proper angle; and the infeed table must be positioned for the proper depth of cut.

---

### A SAFETY REMINDER

**A**lways *unplug the jointer* before making any alignments or adjustments that will bring your hands close to the cutterhead or any other moving parts.

---

*Adjusting the tables* — Although jointer tables are ground flat and parallel at the factory, they don't always stay that way. If the tables were machined too soon after they were cast, they may warp or bow. Moving the jointer cross-country may knock the tables out of alignment. If someone carelessly uses the jointer as a workbench or a step stool and puts a great deal of weight on the ends of the tables, they may become misaligned.

When you purchase your jointer, and periodically thereafter, check that infeed and outfeed tables are perfectly flat and parallel to each other. To determine that the tables are flat, lay a precision straightedge along each of them individually. (*SEE FIGURE 1-7.*) To check that they're parallel, adjust them to the same height, then lay a straightedge across *both* of them. (*SEE FIGURE 1-8.*) If the tables are not flat, have them

**1-7 To check that a jointer table** is flat, lay a precision straightedge across it lengthwise. With a feeler gauge, measure any gaps between the straightedge and the table — they should all be less than .005 inch. If either the infeed or the outfeed table is out of flat by more than .005 inch at any point, have *both* tables ground flat by a professional machine shop. **Note:** The tables must be ground together, attached to their base. If you grind just one, or grind them separately, they may not be properly aligned when you reassemble the jointer.

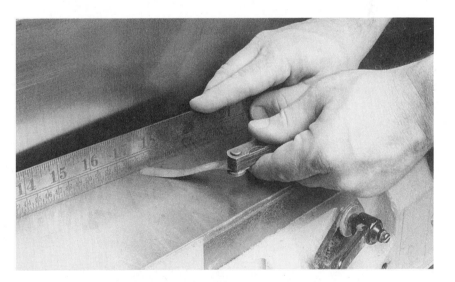

**1-8 When you're satisfied that** the tables are flat, raise or lower the infeed table until it's at the same level as the outfeed table. Lay a straightedge across *both* tables and look for any gaps between the tables and the straightedge. Check at several points — down the middle of the tables, near both edges, and diagonally from corner to corner. Measure any gaps with a feeler gauge — once again, there should be no gap greater than .010 inch. If there is, either adjust the tables parallel or have them machined. **Note:** The straightedge must be long enough to span the length of *both* tables.

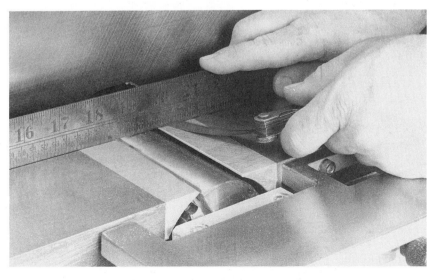

reground. If they are not parallel, clean the ways or follow the instructions in your owner's manual for adjusting them. (SEE FIGURES 1-9 AND 1-10.) If you cannot easily adjust the tables parallel to one another, you will have to have them reground. **Note:** You should also check the jointer fence with a straightedge. It, too, may need grinding.

---

## FOR YOUR INFORMATION

Make sure that your straightedge is true. If it isn't, you will have to have it machined straight before you can accurately check the flatness of the jointer tables. If the straightedge is trustworthy and it shows that the tables aren't flat, call the customer service number listed in the jointer owner's manual. Some manufacturers provide a machining service to regrind their jointer tables.

---

*Setting the knives* — Whenever you change jointer knives, make sure they are set to the proper height, in relation to each other and to the outfeed table. If they

are not set correctly, the jointer won't cut properly. First, the knives must all be set to exactly the same height. When they aren't, only the highest knife will cut, leaving a rough surface with pronounced mill marks. Second, the tips of the knives must be dead even with or just a few thousandths of an inch above the outfeed table at the highest point in their cutting arc. If the knives are set too *high,* the jointer will make a slightly *concave* cut rather than a straight cut. It will also leave a snipe at the end of the board. If they are too *low,* the jointer will make a slightly *tapered* cut, removing more stock at the beginning of the cut than at the end. The stock may also hang up on the outfeed table at the beginning of the cut.

When changing or resetting the knives, do just one knife at a time. The locking bars and locking screws that hold the knives in place exert a great deal of internal stress in the cutterhead. If you take out all the knives and completely release this stress, the cutterhead may be distorted as you put the knives back in. By the time you set the last knife, the first one may be out of alignment due to this distortion. To keep track of which knives you've set and which still need to be done, label them by writing with a grease pencil on the cutterhead, then do them in order.

**1-9 If the tables are out of** parallel, take the jointer apart and thoroughly clean the mating surfaces between the base and the tables — sometimes a buildup of sawdust or grime will affect the alignment. Then put the jointer back together and carefully adjust the *gibs*. Gibs are flat pieces of metal between the mating surfaces that can be loosened or tightened to adjust the fit of the parts. More often than not, when the tables aren't parallel, it's because the gibs are loose. Check the jointer owner's manual for instructions on how to adjust the gibs.

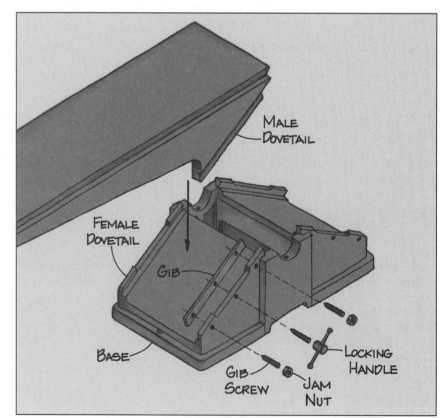

**TRY THIS TRICK**

**I**f you don't have an extra set of knives, and you must take all the knives out at once to sharpen them, just tighten the locking screws *partially* when you put them back in. Once they're set, tighten all the screws a little more. Finally tighten them all completely. By tightening *all* the screws in increments, you can prevent the cutterhead from distorting.

Turn the cutterhead until the first knife is up. Loosen the locking screws and the locking bar, remove the knife, and thoroughly clean the cutterhead groove and the locking bar. If the surface of the locking bar is rough or galled (marred by hard use or overtightening), hone it smooth and flat. (*SEE FIGURE 1-11.*) If the

knife is dull, swap it for a sharp one; then replace the knife and the locking bar in the cutterhead. Tighten the locking screws until the knife is snug, but not so tight that you can't slide the knife back and forth.

Select a 12-inch-long scrap of wood with a straight edge and make two marks on its face ⅛ inch apart and 2 inches from one end. Place the scrap on the outfeed table so it extends over the knife, near one end. The first mark (nearer the cutterhead) must be even with the edge of the table. Using the jack screws, adjust the knife height so it will catch the scrap when you rock the cutterhead forward, and drag it until the second mark is even with the edge — precisely ⅛ inch. (*SEE FIGURE 1-12.*) Repeat at the other end of the knife, then check the knife at the middle. When the knife will drag the scrap ⅛ inch no matter where you position the scrap along the knife's length, tighten the locking screws completely. (*SEE FIGURE 1-13.*)

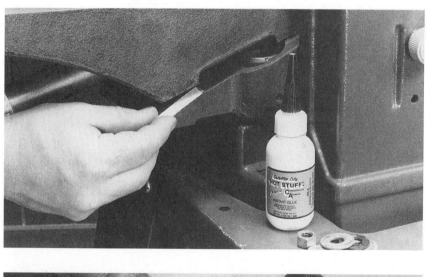

**1-10  If cleaning the mating** surfaces and adjusting the gibs doesn't bring the tables parallel to one another, you may have to insert shims between the tables and the base at one or more points. Brass or steel shim stock, available from most automotive stores, is your best choice. But you can also use paper, playing cards, or cut-up aluminum beverage cans. Use cyanoacrylate adhesive to secure the shim to the jointer base.

**1-11  A rough locking bar may** prevent you from setting a knife accurately. As you tighten the locking screws, the rough surface contacts the knife unevenly and it squirms out of adjustment. To keep this squirming to a minimum, hone the bar smooth and flat on a sharpening stone or a piece of 120-grit sandpaper adhered to a piece of glass.

**1-12  To gauge the knife height,**
use a scrap of wood with two marks
⅛ inch apart. Place the scrap on the
outfeed table so it extends over the
knife. Rock the cutterhead back and
forth while turning the jack screws
to raise or lower the knife. Stop when
the knife just brushes the scrap.
Then position the scrap so the first
mark (nearer the cutterhead) is
even with the edge of the outfeed
table. Rock the cutterhead forward
(toward the infeed table) until the
knife catches the scrap and drags it.
The knife should release the scrap
when the second mark is even with
the edge. If the knife drags the scrap
too far, it's too high — lower the
knife slightly. If the knife doesn't
drag it far enough, it's too low —
raise it slightly.

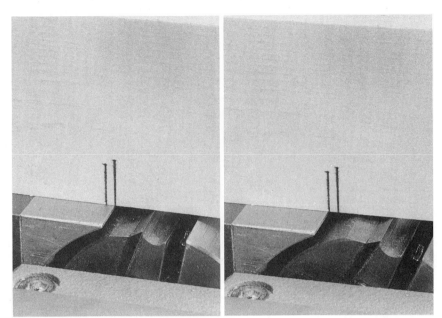

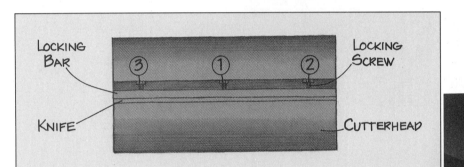

**1-13  When the knife will drag**
the scrap precisely ⅛ inch, no matter where you set the scrap along the
knife's length, tighten the locking
screws on the locking bar. Tighten
the middle screws first, then work
out toward the ends. When they are
all tight, check that the knife hasn't
squirmed out of adjustment. If you
have trouble with the knife squirming, tighten the screws in stages,
turning them in order a little bit at
a time until tight.

## FOR YOUR INFORMATION

**W**hen the knives are set to drag the scrap-wood
gauge ⅛ inch, they are approximately .001 to .003
inch above the table at the highest point of their arc
(depending on the diameter of the cutterhead). This
slight protrusion compensates for *springback.* When
the whirling knives contact the wood, they compress
it slightly as they cut. Immediately after the wood is
cut, the compressed fibers spring back approximately
.002 inch — slightly more in softwoods, less in
hardwoods.

There are also several commercial jigs available to help you set the knives. One of the most popular uses magnets to hold the knife at the proper height while you tighten the locking screws. *(SEE FIGURE 1-14.)*

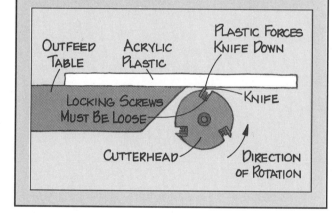

## TRY THIS TRICK

**I**f your jointer doesn't have jack screws or a similar mechanism to raise and lower the knives precisely, loosen the locking screws so the knife slides easily but without any slop. Raise the knife slightly higher than the outfeed table. Place a flat piece of acrylic plastic on the outfeed table so it extends over the entire length of the knife. Rotate the cutterhead *backward* (toward the outfeed table). As you do so, the plastic will push the knife down in the cutterhead to precisely the right height. Tighten the locking screws, then check by rotating the cutterhead again — the knife should barely brush the plastic all along its length.

OUTFEED TABLE    ACRYLIC PLASTIC    PLASTIC FORCES KNIFE DOWN

LOCKING SCREWS MUST BE LOOSE    KNIFE

CUTTERHEAD    DIRECTION OF ROTATION

Once the knives are all at the same height, you must check that they are also at the proper height in relation to the outfeed table. Select a scrap of wood about 36 inches long, joint the edge, and check with a straightedge that the edge is true. If it is, the knives are close. To find out if they are right on the money, joint the edge again and make sure the knives remove the same amount of stock all along the cut. *(SEE FIGURES 1-15 AND 1-16.)*

If the knives are not set correctly to the outfeed table, and your jointer has an adjustable outfeed table, simply move the table up or down until the jointer is cutting properly. Otherwise, you must reset the knives. If the cut is concave and the knives are too *high,* set them to drag the scrap-wood gauge ¹⁄₆₄ to ¹⁄₃₂ inch *less* than ¹⁄₈ inch. If the cut is tapered and the knives are *low,* set them to drag the gauge a little *more.*

**1-14  A magnetic knife-setting jig** holds a jointer knife parallel to and at the same height as the outfeed table. Rotate the cutterhead so the knife is at *top dead center* — the highest point in its arc. Then, with the knife held in place by the magnets, tighten the locking screws.

*Setting the fence angle* — When you simply want to joint a surface straight and true, the fence angle is not critical. But when you wish to joint that surface at a precise angle to another, then the fence position becomes important.

Usually, you want to make one surface square to another. The edges of most boards, for example, are jointed square to their faces. To do this, the jointer fence must be 90 degrees from the table surfaces. Use a trustworthy square to set the fence. *(SEE FIGURE 1-17.)* Don't trust the tilt gauge or the stops; these can creep out of adjustment. When setting the fence to an angle other than 90 degrees, use a combination square, drafting triangles, or a sliding T-bevel.

*Setting the depth of cut* — The depth of cut is controlled by the level of the infeed table — the lower you set the table, the deeper the cut. The proper depth of cut depends on the type of cut you want to make, the stock, and the width of the surface you're cutting.

To remove stock quickly, as when straightening the edge of a badly warped board, set the depth of cut fairly deep — ¹⁄₁₆ to ¹⁄₈ inch. For smooth finishing cuts, set the jointer to cut ¹⁄₁₆ inch deep or less. If you're jointing figured stock, such as curly maple, you may want to set the depth of cut even shallower — 1/32 inch or less — to prevent chipping and tear-out.

When jointing narrow surfaces, you can make deep cuts. But the wider the surface, the shallower your cuts should be. When jointing the full width of the knives, the depth of cut shouldn't be more than 1/16 inch — even less for extremely hard woods. If you cut too wide and deep, the jointer may bog down in the cut or the board may kick back.

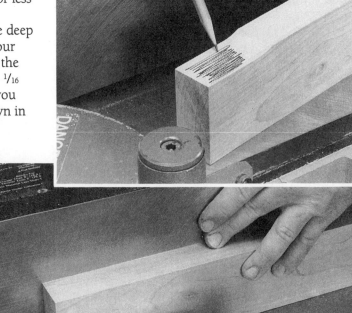

**1-15  To determine if the knives** are set at the proper height, select a scrap about 36 inches long and joint one edge straight. Joint the edge a second time, but stop 1 or 2 inches into the cut. Remove the scrap from the jointer and shade the twice-jointed area with a pencil.

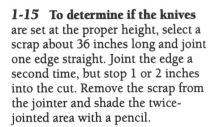

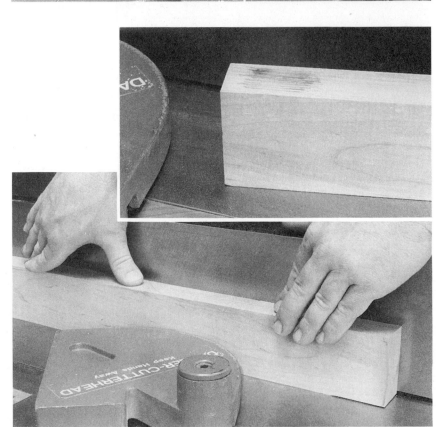

**1-16  Turn the scrap end for end** and joint the same edge again, but this time complete the cut. Inspect the shaded area of the jointed edge. If the pencil marks are just as dark as they were and there is a step where you stopped jointing, the knives are too low (or the outfeed table is too high). If the pencil marks have been removed completely, the knives are too high (or the outfeed table is too low). In either case, you must adjust the level of the outfeed table or reset the knives. When the step is gone and the pencil marks are lighter but still evident (especially in the wood pores), the knives and the outfeed table are in the proper relationship.

**1-17** **Use a square to set the fence** precisely 90 degrees from the tables. For other angles, use a combination square, drafting triangles, or a sliding T-bevel — whichever is the most convenient. Always gauge the angle near the cutterhead. That way, even if the fence has a slight twist, the stock will be at the proper angle when it passes over the cutterhead.

## COMMON JOINTING TECHNIQUES

When using the jointer, there are a few simple guidelines to follow:

■ Clean the wood before you joint it, removing any sand or dirt with a wire brush. If you don't, the knives will dull quickly.

■ Never joint plywood, painted wood, or used lumber. Plywood and painted wood will quickly dull the knives, sometimes in a single pass. Used lumber may have nails, screws, and other fasteners imbedded in it that will chip the knives.

■ Always keep the stock pressed firmly against the tables and the fence.

■ As much as possible, cut *downhill* so the knives shave the wood grain rather than dig into it. (SEE FIGURE 1-18.)

■ Feed the stock slowly and steadily. If you feed too fast, the jointer will leave mill marks. If you stop in the middle of a cut, the knives may burn the wood. (SEE FIGURE 1-19.)

■ To keep your hands away from the cutterhead, use push sticks, push blocks, and push shoes to feed the stock whenever practical. (SEE FIGURE 1-20.)

■ Don't joint boards that are too short or too thin to handle safely. The stock should be at least 10 inches

**1-18** **Before jointing a board,** inspect it to see which way the grain runs. Whenever possible, feed the wood so the knives cut *downhill,* shaving the grain rather than digging into it. If you feed the wood in the opposite direction, the grain may chip or tear. Oftentimes you will not be able to tell which way to feed the wood. In this case, take your best guess and listen for the telltale snicking or popping sounds that indicate the jointer is chipping the grain. If the wood grain chips, reverse the feed direction. If the grain still chips, reduce the feed rate and the depth of cut. Also, check that your knives are sharp.

FEED DIRECTION

**RIGHT — PLANER SHAVES THE WOOD GRAIN**

**WRONG — PLANER DIGS INTO GRAIN**

long and ¼ inch thick. It's difficult to make accurate cuts in small boards without bringing your hands dangerously close to the cutterhead. Furthermore, the stock may break apart or kick back. (*See Figure 1-21.*)

■ Make sure the chip chute is clear. If you have a dust collection attachment for the jointer, hook it up and turn on the vacuum. Jointers generate fine dust as well as a *lot* of wood shavings.

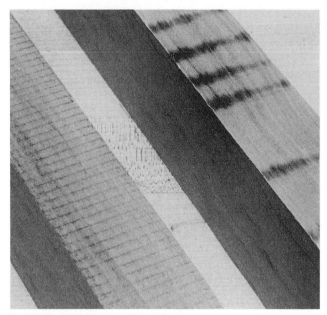

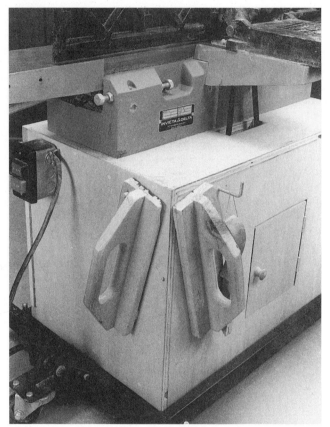

**1-19  Because the jointer knives** travel in a circle, the jointer doesn't cut a truly flat surface. Instead, it cuts a series of arcs. If you feed the wood too fast, the arcs or *mill marks* (*left*) are far apart and become visible. Feed the wood slowly so the arcs are closer together and the surface appears flat. But don't feed too slowly, or stop in the middle of a cut — if the knives dwell too long in one spot, they may burn the wood (*right*).

**1-20  Keep push blocks and push** shoes within easy reach when making a cut. Many craftsmen prefer to hang them right on the jointer stand.

**1-21  It's unwise to joint short or** thin boards — accurate cuts are difficult to make, and your hands may come too close to the cutterhead. If you must joint small stock, attach it to the bottom of a push block with double-faced carpet tape. This will give you more control and keep your hands out of danger.

*Jointing faces* — Before jointing the face of a board, inspect the wood. If it's cupped, turn the cup *down* — this will make the wood more stable. If the cup is up, the wood may rock. Place the wood on the infeed table and pass it slowly across the cutterhead, using push shoes or push blocks *in both hands*. Keep the wood pressed against the infeed table just in front of the cutterhead, and — as soon as possible — against the outfeed table. (*See Figure 1-22.*)

*Jointing edges* — Before jointing an edge, inspect the board to make sure you have a flat face to hold against the fence. If not, joint the face first. Also check if the board is crooked. If so, joint the edge with the concave side of the crook down. As you feed the board, keep it pressed firmly against the fence. (*See Figure 1-23.*)

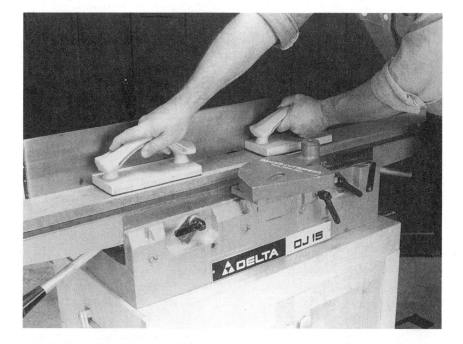

**1-22  If the knives are properly** set, you'll get a more accurate cut by transferring *most* of the pressure to the outfeed table as soon as enough stock has passed across the cutterhead. However, continue to apply some pressure to the infeed table, just in front of the cutterhead. This will help control vibration and chatter.

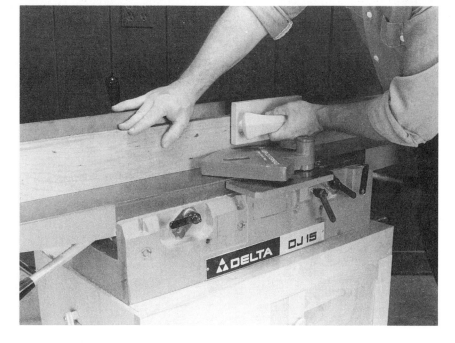

**1-23  Edges are jointed by the** same rules that apply to jointing a face — as soon as possible, transfer *most* (but not all) of the pressure to the outfeed table. However, you must also keep the board pressed flat against the fence. Oftentimes, an inexperienced craftsman applies too much pressure to the table and not enough to the fence. As a result, the bottom edge of the board creeps away from the fence and the jointed edge is not square to the face.

## TRY THIS TRICK

If you don't have a jointer, you can true edges on a router table with the simple jig shown. Mount a 1-inch-diameter straight bit in the router and position the jig so that the outfeed (laminate-covered) surface is tangent to the cutting arc of the bit. Feed the edge of the stock slowly and steadily across the bit. If you get a concave cut, move the jig toward the bit slightly. If the cut is tapered, move the jig away from the bit. When the jig is positioned precisely, you can joint perfectly straight edges.

STRAIGHTEDGE

VARIABLE TO FIT ROUTER TABLE

1¼" DIA

INFEED SIDE

½"

PLASTIC LAMINATE

3"

OUTFEED SIDE

*Jointing bevels and chamfers* — When you must joint the edge of a board at an angle other than 90 degrees, tilt the fence *toward* the table, if possible. As explained earlier, the acute angle cradles the stock and prevents it from slipping. This helps you make an accurate cut. When you must tilt the fence away from the table, it's often necessary to attach a guide to the jointer tables to keep the stock from slipping. (*See Figure 1-24.*)

*Jointing ends* — Although it's an unusual operation, every now and then you may have to joint end grain. This is hard on the knives, and unless you take precautions, the stock will split as you finish the cut. To keep from dulling the cutting edges, take very shallow cuts — 1/32 inch or less. Back up the wood to prevent splitting; or, if you can't do that, joint the end partway and reverse the cut. (*See Figures 1-25 and 1-26.*)

**1-24  When jointing at an angle** other than 90 degrees, you'll find it's easier to control the stock if you tilt the fence *toward* the tables. If you must tilt the fence *away* from the tables (as shown), attach stops to the tables with double-faced tape. These serve as auxiliary guides and prevent the stock from slipping as you joint it.

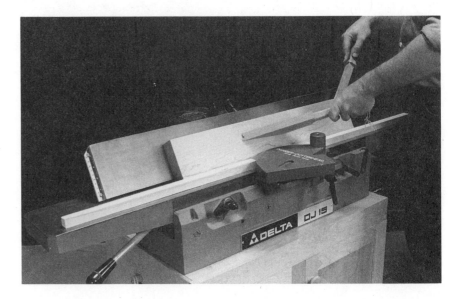

---

### A SAFETY REMINDER

Some of the jointer techniques that you may find in older books and manuals, such as tapering legs and cutting tenons, are now considered *dangerous*. They stretch the capacity of the jointer beyond what it was designed to do. There are safer and better tools in your shop to accomplish these tasks. Tapering, for example, should be done on a table saw, a band saw, or — as you will see in the next chapter — a planer. And it's much easier to cut tenons on a table saw, a lathe, a drill press, or a router table. The jointer is best used for jointing.

---

**1-25  To joint end grain, first** make sure the board is wide enough (10 inches or more) to cut safely. It shouldn't be too long, either, or it will stick up so far above the fence that you will have trouble controlling it. Make extremely shallow cuts (1/32 inch or less) and back up the trailing edge with a scrap. If you don't back up the edge, it will split out, as shown in the inset.

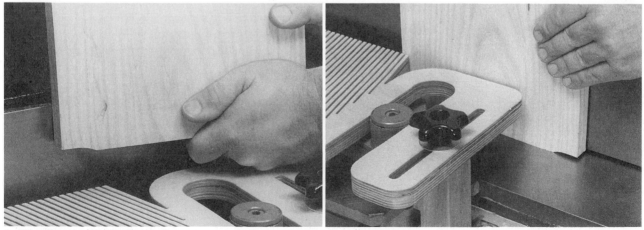

**1-26  If you can't back up the** trailing edge, prevent the edge from splitting by jointing in two steps. Joint the end partway, stopping the cut after 1 or 2 inches. Reverse the board edge for edge and finish the cut.

## JOINTER MAINTENANCE

Performing several simple chores will keep your jointer in good working order. Remember to *unplug the jointer* before performing any of these:

■ Keep the knives free of wood pitch — pitch can interfere with the cutting action. Frequently, when the knives of a jointer seem dull, they only need to be cleaned. Spray a rag with oven cleaner and wipe the pitch off the knives. You can spray the knives with silicone to prevent pitch build-up. Mineral spirits, naphtha, or acetone also dissolve pitch.

■ Wax and buff the tables and the fence, using ordinary furniture paste wax. This will clean and lubricate the surfaces, helping the wood to slide smoothly across them.

■ Periodically (once every year or so) clean the jointer thoroughly. Remove the tables from the base and clean the gunk that accumulates in the ways or tracks. Blow or brush away all wood chips and sawdust, then reassemble and realign the jointer.

■ After every five hours of operating time — or sooner, if you think the jointer isn't cutting as well as it might — touch up the knives with a sharpening stone and a slip stone. You don't have to remove the knives from the cutterhead; you can touch them up in place. (*SEE FIGURE 1-27.*)

■ When you can see a bright, white line reflected from the cutting edges of your knife, it's time to have it sharpened. The reflection is caused by the *land,* a rounded spot that develops on the bevel, just behind the tip, as the knife grows dull. (*SEE FIGURE 1-28.*) It's best to keep a spare set of sharp knives on hand for this eventuality. That way, you can replace the dull knives one at a time with sharp ones. You never have to remove all the knives from your cutterhead at once, and the jointer doesn't sit useless while you're waiting for the knives to be sharpened.

**Note:** Unless you have water-cooled grinding wheels, your jointer knives should be professionally sharpened. It takes an extraordinarily long time to sharpen these knives by hand with oilstones or waterstones, and ordinary high-speed abrasives may leave microscopic heat fractures (caused by friction) in the cutting edges. The knives will cut well at first, but the sharp edges won't last long.

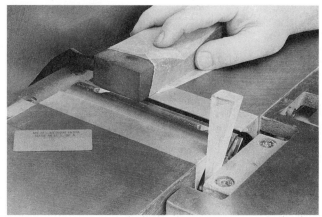

**1-27  To touch up the jointer** knives, rotate the cutterhead until the bevel of one knife is horizontal, and hold it in place with a small wooden wedge. Lower the infeed table even with the bevel. Wrap a fine stone in wax paper, letting one end protrude about ½ inch. Lay the stone on the infeed table so the exposed end contacts the knife bevel. Check that the stone rests flat on the bevel — if not, adjust the position of the cutterhead or the infeed table. Apply a little oil to the stone, and slide it back and forth along the length of the knife. Carefully wipe away any oil left on the knife or the cutterhead. Repeat for each knife.

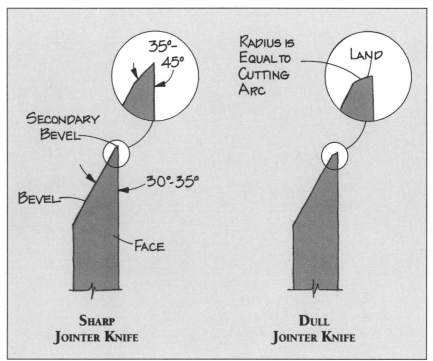

**1-28 A sharp jointer knife has a** *bevel* ground on the back of the *face.* The angle between the bevel and the face is usually 30 to 35 degrees. Some craftsmen prefer to draw a sharp knife across a fine stone once or twice before they install it, holding the bevel about 5 to 10 degrees from the surface of the stone. This produces a tiny *secondary bevel* and extends the life of the cutting edge. As the cutting edge wears, the secondary bevel (if there is one) disappears and a rounded spot or *land* develops in the bevel. This land burnishes the wood and interferes with the cutting action.

## Try This Trick

If you work mostly with extremely hard woods, such as oak and maple, and you have problems with chipped and torn grain, have a sharpening service grind a 3- to 5-degree *face bevel* in your jointer knives, in addition to the ordinary bevel. The optimum angle at which the knife attacks the wood — called a *rake angle* — is steeper for hardwoods than it is for softwoods. The rake angle on most jointers is a compromise so you can cut both types of wood, but it's not the best possible angle for either one. A face bevel makes the rake angle steeper, and you'll get smoother cuts in hardwood. **Note:** As the rake angle grows steeper, the jointer requires more power. If you have face bevels ground in the knives, you may also need a more powerful motor.

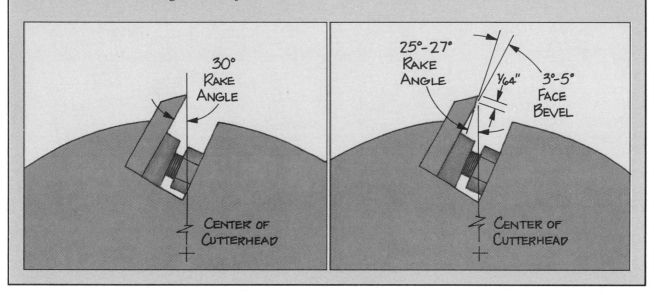

# JOINTER SAFETY ACCESSORIES

The key to using the jointer safely is to keep your hands *away from the cutterhead*, yet remain in control of the stock you are cutting. Push sticks, push blocks, and push shoes help you do this, by extending your reach without bringing your fingers close to the whirling knives. Push blocks and push shoes even function as shields — the bases provide a barrier between you and disaster should your hands slip or the stock kick back. Here are two additional safety accessories:

**1**   **The *long push block* is an** extended, two-fisted version of an ordinary push block. It's designed to be used with *both* hands, and it is useful for feeding short boards (under 18 inches long) and other workpieces that would be awkward to feed with two separate push blocks.

**2**   **The wider the board, the** more difficult it is to keep it flat against the fence as you joint the edge. The *jointer featherboard* attaches to the jointer base and presses the wood against the fence over both the infeed and outfeed tables. It adjusts to accommodate most sizes of stock. Adapt the length of the mounting posts and the shape of the featherboard to your jointer. They must not interfere with the cutterhead guard or the table adjustment. Make the featherboard from Baltic birch plywood (for strength), and tap holes in the jointer base to attach the mounting posts.

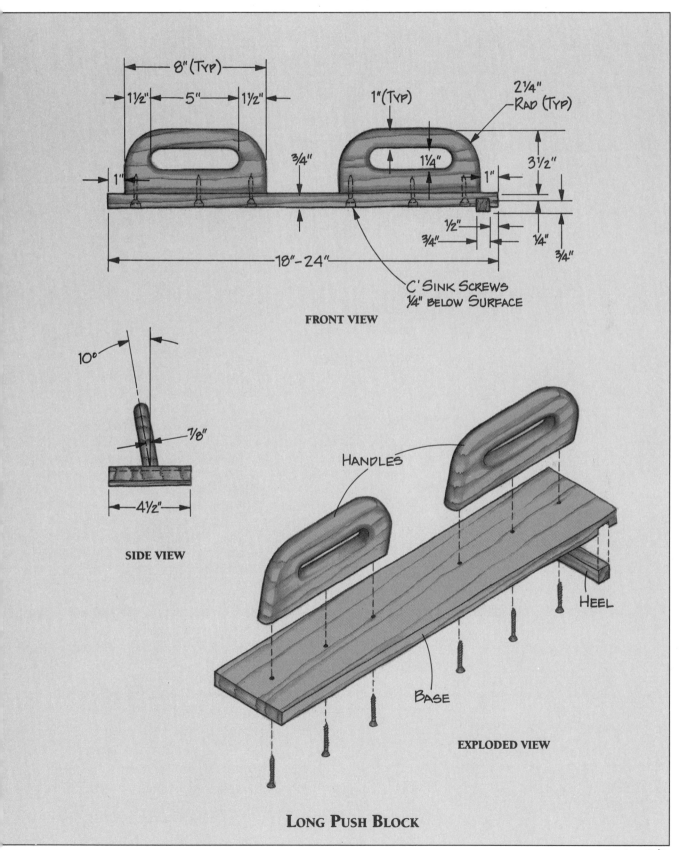

8" (Typ)

1½" — 5" — 1½"

1" (Typ)

2¼"
Rad (Typ)

¾"

1¼"

3½"

1"

1"

½"

¾"

¼"

¾"

18"–24"

C'Sink Screws
¼" below Surface

**FRONT VIEW**

10°

⅞"

4½"

**SIDE VIEW**

Handles

Heel

Base

**EXPLODED VIEW**

## Long Push Block

(continued) ▷

# JOINTER SAFETY ACCESSORIES — CONTINUED

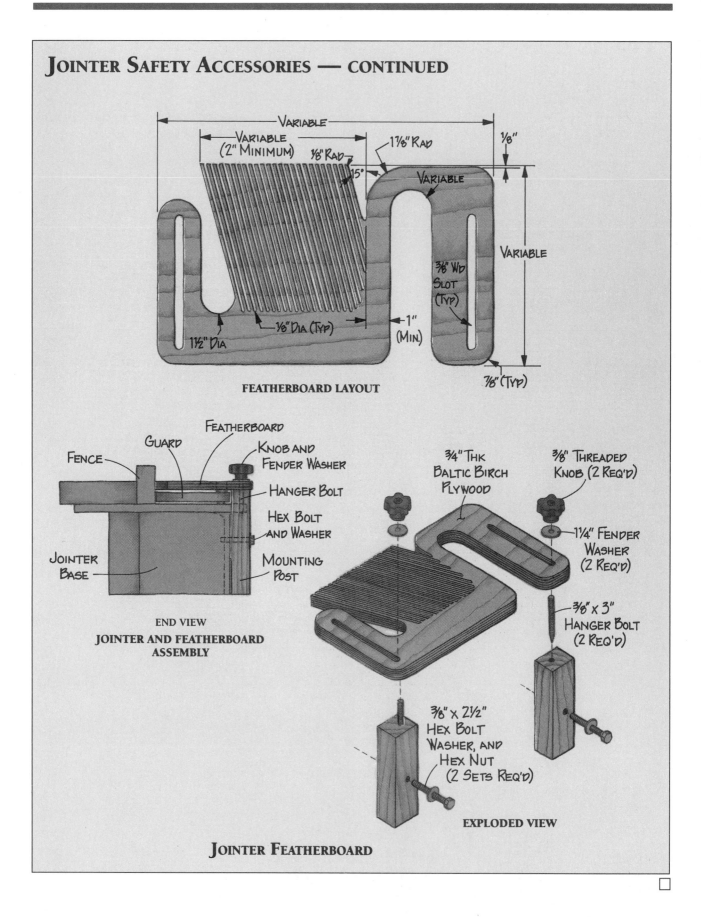

**FEATHERBOARD LAYOUT**

**END VIEW**
**JOINTER AND FEATHERBOARD**
**ASSEMBLY**

**EXPLODED VIEW**

**JOINTER FEATHERBOARD**

# 2

# Using the Thickness Planer

Superficially, a thickness planer resembles a jointer. Both power tools have a cutterhead with several long knives and a long, flat work surface. Both cut a smooth surface when you feed rough stock through them. Consequently, novice woodworkers are apt to assume they do some of the same tasks, but nothing could be further from the truth.

As we saw in the first chapter, the primary purpose of a jointer is to *true* boards, cutting the surfaces straight and flat. You can also use a jointer to cut a true surface at a precise angle to another. A thickness planer, on the other hand, simply cuts one surface parallel to another, and in doing so, reduces the thickness of the stock. And that's it — the planer does not cut straight surfaces or flat surfaces, just *parallel* surfaces.

# Choosing a Thickness Planer

Although it may not be as versatile as other machines, a planer is indispensable if you want to do any serious woodworking. No other power tool will thickness lumber as accurately and as easily.

## HOW A THICKNESS PLANER WORKS

To use a planer, first adjust the distance between the table or *bed* and the *cutterhead* by turning the *thickness adjustment.* On some planers, the bed moves up and down; on others, the cutterhead moves. In either case, the thickness of the planed stock is determined by the distance from the bed to the *knives* in the cutterhead. This adjustment also determines the depth of cut — the amount of stock that will be removed from a board in a single pass through the machine.

Turn on the planer and feed a board into the infeed opening. As it travels past the *anti-kickback pawls,* a serrated *infeed roller* grabs the wood, passes it under the cutterhead, and then on to the *outfeed roller.* The knives shave the surface of the wood as it passes by, and a *chip breaker* — situated between the infeed roller and the cutterhead — breaks up the shavings so they can be easily evacuated. On some planers, a *pressure bar* between the cutterhead and the outfeed roller holds the board firmly against the bed as it's cut. There may also be *bed rollers* directly under the infeed and outfeed rollers to reduce the friction between the board and the bed.

The *motor* in the planer usually drives both the cutterhead and the feed rollers, although some planers have separate feed and cutterhead motors. On some small planers, the motor is mounted over the cutterhead; on most, it's mounted beneath the bed in the *stand.* The *on/off switch* is always located on the infeed side of the machine where it can be easily reached as you're feeding the wood. (*See Figure 2-1.*)

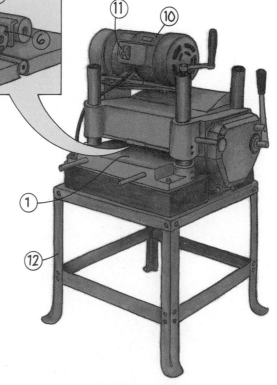

**2-1  A thickness planer's sturdy** metal **bed** (1) guides the wood under the **cutterhead** (2). An **infeed roller** (3) and an **outfeed roller** (4) feed the stock, while a **pressure bar** (5) keeps it flat against the bed. As the **knives** (6) in the cutterhead cut the wood, a **chip breaker** (7) breaks up the shavings and directs them away from the stock. **Bed rollers** (8) keep the stock gliding smoothly over the bed, while **anti-kickback pawls** (9) prevent it from kicking back. A **motor** (10) turns both the cutterhead and the feed rollers, and the **on/off switch** (11) is located near the infeed opening. The machine usually rests on a **stand** (12).

## TYPES OF PLANERS

Thickness planers come in all sizes, from tiny bench-top units with 7-inch-wide cutterheads to huge 48-inch-wide floor models. In addition to the variety of sizes, there are also four types of planers:

■ *Stationary planers* are heavily constructed, often weighing several hundred pounds. On some models, the planer housing extends to the floor and serves as a stand. *(SEE FIGURE 2-2.)*

■ *Portable planers* are light-duty, small-capacity machines. They weigh less than a hundred pounds and have no stand, making them easy to move about. *(SEE FIGURE 2-3.)*

■ *Convertible jointer/planers* use the same cutterhead for jointing and planing. Pass the work over the cutterhead to joint it, and under the cutterhead to plane it. *(SEE FIGURE 2-4.)*

■ *Planer/molders* combine the functions of a planer and a molder. You can replace the straight knives in the cutterhead with shaped cutters to produce moldings. *(SEE FIGURE 2-5.)*

**2-2  Stationary thickness planers** are massive machines that rest either on the floor or on sturdy stands. Even the smallest units may weigh several hundred pounds.

**2-3  Although portable planers** are built along the same lines as their stationary cousins, they are made light enough to carry easily. You can store one under a bench until it's time to do some planing, then attach it to a stand temporarily. *Photo courtesy of Ryobi America Corp.*

**2-4  Although jointers and planers** don't perform the same operations, you can combine their functions in a single machine. This tool uses the same motor to turn a jointer and a planer cutterhead. There are also combination machines that use the same cutterhead for jointing and planing — pass the stock over the cutterhead to joint it, and under the cutterhead to plane it. *Photo courtesy of Makita U.S.A., Inc.*

**2-5  A few planers let you mount** shaped molding knives in place of the straight planing knives in the cutterhead. Not only can you create moldings on the thickness planer, you can make decorative shapes in the middle of wide boards. Some Belsaw machines do triple duty as a thickness sander. *Photo courtesy of Belsaw Co.*

## PLANER FEATURES

When purchasing a thickness planer, consider these features:

*Maximum width of cut* — Most thickness planers will cut boards only as wide as the cutterhead. (The exception to this rule is the open-sided Williams and Hussey planer, which will plane boards twice as wide as the cutterhead — *SEE FIGURE 2-6.*) How wide a cutterhead do you need? As wide as the widest boards you customarily work. For most woodworkers, this is 12 inches — boards wider than that have become very rare. Manufacturers beat their chests about their 15-inch and 18-inch machines, but practically, the extra capacity adds more weight (a good thing) and expense (a bad thing) than it does versatility. There is little advantage to larger planers unless you consider machines that are at least 24 inches wide. These enable you to plane wide, edge-glued panels and tabletops. However, you must have a large shop and glue up a lot of wide stock to justify the expense of one of these monsters.

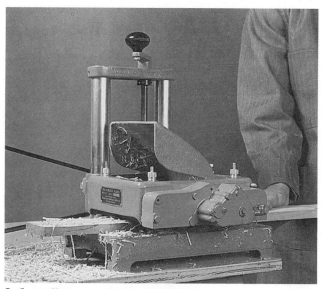

**2-6 Williams and Hussey makes** a small, open-sided portable planer. The cutterhead is very narrow — just 7 inches wide — but the unique design allows you to plane boards that are wider than the cutterhead. Feed wide stock through once to plane a portion of the board; then turn it end for end and feed it through again to plane the remainder. In this manner, you can plane boards up to 14 inches wide. *Photo courtesy of Williams and Hussey Machine Co., Inc.*

*Maximum thickness* — The maximum thickness of the stock you can cut is determined by how far apart you can adjust the bed and the cutterhead. Here again, remember the size of the wood you work. You can't purchase cabinet-grade lumber thicker than 16/4 (sixteen-quarters) unless you special-order it from a sawyer, so a planer with a 4-inch capacity will likely serve all your needs. Some craftsmen like to plane stock on edge when they need boards that are precisely the same width, and for this operation you may need a machine that opens up more than 4 inches. However, there are other tools in your shop that will perform this task just as well as a planer, so this shouldn't be an important factor in your consideration.

*Motor type and horsepower* — Give careful consideration to the motor type and horsepower: They affect the performance of the tool enormously. It requires a lot of power to make wide cuts, and if the planer is underpowered, it will bog down. Your thicknessing chores will take longer, and the motor may eventually burn out. You need *at least* 2 horsepower for a small planer; 3 horsepower is better. Additionally, you should look for an *induction* motor. Some small planers, portable models in particular, often have high-speed *universal* motors. Although these may be rated at 2 horsepower, the rating is deceptive because a universal motor is rated using a different method than induction motors. They are actually much less powerful than similarly rated low-speed induction motors. Nor will they last as long under continuous use. Furthermore, a universal motor is much louder than an induction motor — no small consideration when you must spend long periods of time planing. *(SEE FIGURE 2-7.)*

*Maximum depth of cut* — On most small and medium-size planers, the depth of cut is mechanically limited to $^3/_{16}$ inch or less — you can only reduce the thickness of the stock by $^3/_{16}$ inch in one pass. Practically, the depth of cut may be further limited by the horsepower of the motor. On some portable planers, it's difficult to cut more than $^1/_{32}$ inch deep when planing a wide, hard board. If you don't have the power required to remove a respectable amount of stock from the wood with each pass, you might spend a lot more time planing than you need to.

*Cutterhead speed and feed rate* — The cutterhead speed for most planers falls between 4,000 and 7,000 rpm — lower for planers with three-knife cutterheads, higher for those with only two knives. The feed rate varies between 12 and 30 feet per minute (fpm). The most important number, however, is the number of

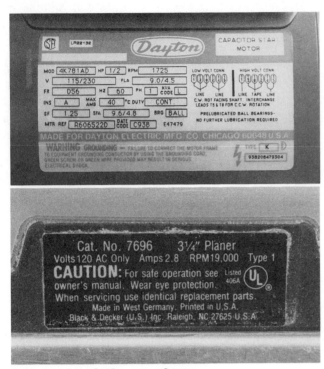

**2-7  To identify the type of motor**
in a power tool, inspect the label on
the motor and find the speed (rpm).
Induction motors almost always turn
at either 1,725 rpm or 3,450 rpm.
Universal motors run at higher
speeds.

cuts per inch (cpi) that the planer makes. The more
cuts per inch, the smoother the planed surface will
be. To find the cpi, first multiply the number of
knives (K) in the cutterhead by the speed (rpm) —
this will give you the cuts per minute. Also multiply
the feed rate (fpm) times 12 to convert it to inches
per minute. Then divide the cuts per minute by the
inches per minute:

$$cpi = (rpm \times K) \div (fpm \times 12)$$

A planer should deliver at least 40 cpi to leave a
respectable surface. The better machines deliver
between 60 and 100 cpi.

Some planers have a *variable* feed rate. You can
change the speed of the rollers either by changing
belts or gears, or — in the Shopsmith planer — by
electronically varying the speed of the feed motor.
This handy feature enables you to change the cpi for
rough and finish cuts. Use a high feed rate for rough
cuts to remove stock quickly, then finish with a low
feed rate for an ultrasmooth surface. You can also
switch to a low feed rate to reduce chipping when
planing hard or figured wood. (*See Figure 2-8.*)

*Cutterhead diameter* — The larger the cutterhead
diameter, the more inertia it has when running. This
makes it less likely to bog down when planing boards
with knots or uneven grain. Also, the cutting arc of
the knives is larger and the planed surface will be
smoother. On the other hand, it takes a lot of horse-

**2-8  The Shopsmith planer's feed**
rate is variable from 7 to 19 fpm —
simply turn the speed control dial
until you're getting the cut you want.
You can also remove the feed motor

and replace it with a hand crank if
you need an even slower feed rate.
This feature allows you to plane
burls, curls, and even end grain.

power to crank a massive cutterhead up to running speed. And the larger the cutterhead diameter, the farther apart the feed rollers must be. If the feed rollers are too far apart, thin stock may vibrate as it passes under the cutterhead, producing a rippled surface. For these reasons, machines with larger cutterheads are generally better for rough work; those with smaller cutterheads are preferred for fine work.

*Construction* — The sheer weight of the planer also affects its operation. As the long knives slam into the wood over 10,000 times a minute, they create enormous vibrations. Heavy castings and other thick metal components help to absorb these vibrations. If you have a lot of planing to do, the heavier machines cut more accurately, run quieter, and last longer.

# PLANER KNOW-HOW

Many craftsmen consider the thickness planer a simple machine, requiring no real technique — just feed rough wood in one side and you get smooth stock out the other. Well, this is true to a certain extent — but the planer has to be properly set up before it will work this easily.

### PLANER ALIGNMENT AND ADJUSTMENT

*Leveling the bed* — The planer bed must be perfectly flat and parallel to the cutterhead. If it isn't, the wood won't feed properly and it won't be cut to a uniform thickness. To check that it's flat, lower the bed (or raise the cutterhead) as far as you can. If your planer

has bed rollers, lower these rollers beneath the surface. Lay a long precision straightedge across the table in several different positions. In each position, measure any gaps between the straightedge and the bed with a feeler gauge. (SEE FIGURE 2-9.) If the bed is more than .010 inch out of flat lengthwise or .005 inch widthwise, have it machined flat.

When you're satisfied that the bed is flat, check that it's parallel to the cutterhead, using a hardwood block as a gauge. (SEE FIGURE 2-10.) If the bed is not parallel, check your owner's manual. Depending on the machine, you may have to adjust threaded rods, gears, or gibs to realign the bed with the cutterhead.

*Adjusting the bed roller height* — If your machine is equipped with bed rollers, these must be set high enough to reduce the friction between the bed and the stock that passes across it. If they're too high, however, the wood won't rest firmly on the bed as it passes under the cutterhead. It may vibrate or chatter, and the planed surface will be uneven. The knives will cut *snipes* in the ends of the boards. (SEE FIGURE 2-11.)

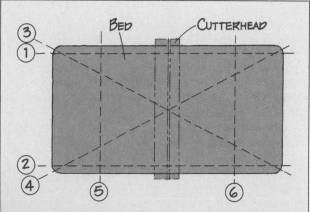

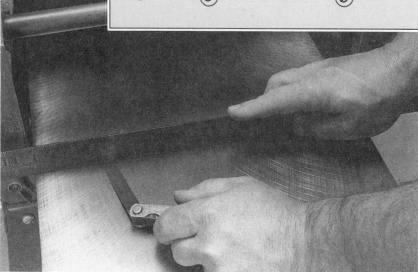

**2-9  Using a precision straight-**edge, check the flatness of the planer bed in six different positions — lengthwise along each edge, along both diagonals, and widthwise near each end. Measure any gaps between the straightedge and the bed with a feeler gauge. When checking lengthwise and diagonally, there should be no gaps greater than .010 inch. When checking widthwise, there should be no gaps greater than .005 inch. **Note:** Make sure your straightedge is perfectly straight. You may need to have it machined before you can use it to measure the flatness of your planer bed.

**2-10  To check that the bed and** cutterhead are parallel, place a block of hardwood on the bed under the cutterhead. Rotate the cutterhead so none of the knives is directly over the block, and raise the bed (or lower the cutterhead) until the cutterhead just touches the block. You should be able to pass the block under the cutterhead with just a little resistance. Do this at both ends of the cutterhead and at several points along its length. The resistance should be the same in all positions. If it isn't — if the block is tighter or looser at some locations than at others — adjust the level of the bed.

**2-11  When the bed rollers are** set too high or the feed rollers don't press down hard enough against the stock, the planer may leave a *snipe* in the ends of the boards — an area several inches long that's a fraction of an inch thinner than the rest of the stock.

**2-12  To find the height of the bed** rollers above the bed, lay a straight-edge across them near one edge of the bed. Measure the gap between the straightedge and the bed with a feeler gauge, then repeat for the opposite edge. The gap should be between .002 inch and .007 inch no matter where you measure it — if not, adjust the level of the rollers. If you use your planer mostly to surface rough lumber, set the rollers fairly high — .005 to .007 inch above the bed. If you also make finishing cuts or plane thin stock, keep the rollers low — .002 to .003 inch.

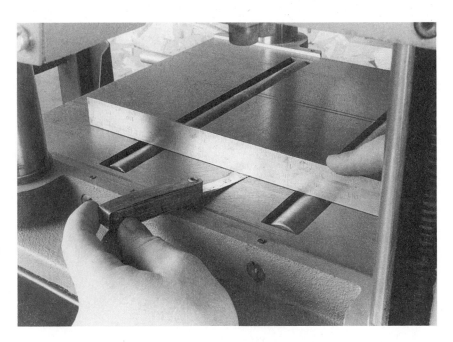

Lay a straightedge across both the infeed and out-feed bed rollers and measure the gap between the straightedge and the bed. (*SEE FIGURE 2-12.*) It should be between .002 and .007 inch. If it isn't, raise or lower the rollers to make it so.

*Adjusting the feed roller pressure* — Both the infeed and outfeed rollers must hold the wood securely on the bed — if they're too loose, they may slip. Additionally, the boards may lift up and the planer will cut snipes in the ends. However, they must not press down so hard that the wood won't feed easily or that the serrated infeed roller bites into the wood surface.

Finding the proper amount of pressure requires some experimentation. Loosen the roller pressure until the rollers are barely pressing down on the wood. Then slowly and evenly increase the feed pressure as you make test cuts and watch for problems. (*SEE FIGURE 2-13.*) When the wood feeds evenly without slipping or sniping, and the infeed roller does not mar the wood, you've found the correct pressure.

## FOR YOUR INFORMATION

**F**eed roller pressure also depends on the type of cut you're making. Deep, rough cuts require more pressure; shallow finish cuts need less. If you make both types of cuts on your planer, find an adjustment that works acceptably for both.

*Setting the knives* — Setting the knives on a planer requires the same technique as setting them on a jointer, with one exception. On a jointer, you have to set the knives to the same height and in the proper relationship to the outfeed table. On a planer, you have to set the knives to the same height — period.

Most planers come with a knife-setting gauge to help you adjust the knives to the same height. If you find this difficult to use, you can make your own or purchase a commercial knife-setting jig. (*SEE FIGURES 2-14 AND 2-15.*) Set just one knife at a time; don't loosen all the locking screws or remove all the knives from the cutterhead at once. When you have adjusted a knife to the proper height, tighten the screws in the locking bar in order, starting at the middle and working toward the ends. If the knife squirms out of adjustment as you tighten the screws, check the surface of the locking bar. If it's rough or scarred, hone it smooth on a flat stone.

*Adjusting the pressure bar* — If the feed rollers on your planer are very far apart, your planer will likely

have a pressure bar. This keeps the whirling knives from lifting the stock off the bed when the rollers are too far away to do so. The pressure bar must be even with the knives at the lowest point in their cutting arc. If it's too high, the stock will chatter and vibrate as it's cut; too low, and the stock will jam under the bar. For this reason, it's wise to check the position of the pressure bar every time you set the knives. (*SEE FIGURE 2-16.*)

## A SAFETY REMINDER

**R**emember to *unplug the planer* before making any adjustment that will bring your hand inside the planer housing or close to the cutterhead.

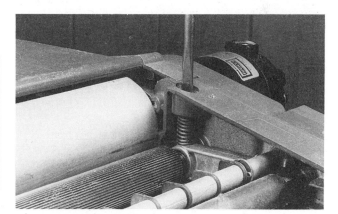

**2-13 On most planers,** compression springs press the feed rollers down against the wood as it travels through the machine. To increase or decrease the roller pressure, turn the screws that compress the springs, rotating each screw the same amount to keep the pressure even. If you suspect the feed roller pressure isn't even — if one end of a roller seems to lift more easily than the other or the stock is pulled to one side as it feeds — back the screws off completely, then tighten them until they just begin to compress the springs. At this point, the pressure will be much too light but fairly even. Increase the pressure slowly and evenly from this point until the planer is feeding and cutting properly. **Note:** Be careful not to collapse the springs completely; you may damage your planer.

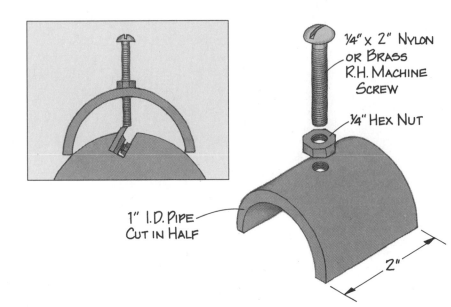

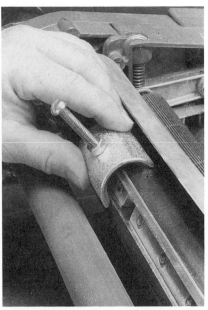

¼" x 2" Nylon or Brass R.H. Machine Screw

¼" Hex Nut

1" I.D. Pipe Cut in Half

2"

**2-14  If the cutterhead in your** planer has leveling screws or another device to set the height of the knives, you can make this device to simplify the job. Loosen the locking screws and place the gauge so it straddles one end of the knife. Raise the knife until it just touches the end of the machine screw in the gauge. Do this again at the other end of the knife and at several points in the middle. When you're satisfied that the entire length of the knife is at the same height, tighten the locking screws. Repeat for the remaining knives. **Note:** Adjust the height of the set-screws so the knives will be even with the bottom of the pressure bar when at the lowest point in their cutting arc. If your planer doesn't have a pressure bar, the height of the screws is not critical, as long as you don't raise the knives so far that they may hit the bed.

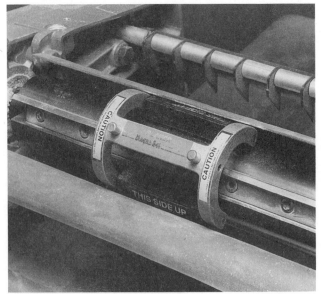

**2-15  If your planer cutterhead** doesn't have knife-leveling devices, a commercial knife-setting jig may be a good investment. The jig shown uses magnets to hold the knives at the proper height while you tighten the screws in the locking bars.

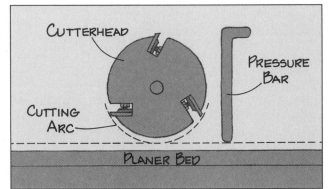

CUTTERHEAD

PRESSURE BAR

CUTTING ARC

PLANER BED

**2-16  If your planer has a** pressure bar, it's wise to check its position every time you set the knives. To do this, plane a scrap of wood, turn off the machine, and — without changing the thickness adjustment — slide the scrap under the bar. There should be a light friction fit. If the fit is too loose, lower the bar. If it's too tight, raise the bar. **Note:** In some machines, the level of the pressure bar may be fixed. If this is the case, you will have to raise or lower the knives.

## PLANING TECHNIQUES

Before you plane a board, clean it with a wire brush and inspect it for imbedded staples and other fasteners. *Never* plane used lumber; if you hit an imbedded nail or screw it will ruin the knives. Don't plane stock that's any shorter than twice the distance between the feed rollers — it won't feed properly and may kick back. When planing long stock, use a roller stand to help support the wood as it feeds out of the planer.

### FOR YOUR INFORMATION

**I**f the stock is cupped or warped, true the stock on a jointer before planing it. Remember, a planer will *not* straighten or flatten a surface — refer to "How to Properly Prepare Wood" on page 38.

Adjust the depth of cut for the type of cut, the wood species, the wood grain, and the width of the stock. If the machine has a variable feed, also set the feed rate for these factors.

*Type of cut* — When surfacing rough lumber or planing to thickness, you want to remove material as quickly as possible. Adjust the depth of cut as deep as *practicable*. On most small planers this will be about $1/8$ inch, but it could be considerably less depending on the horsepower of the motor. Set the feed rate as high as you can — again, this will depend on the available power. If you adjust the depth of cut too deep or the feed rate too high, the machine will bog down as you cut.

As the stock approaches the desired thickness, you want to switch from rough to fine cuts so the finished surface will be as smooth as possible. Set the depth of cut very shallow — $1/32$ to $1/64$ inch — so the planer just shaves the wood. Also reduce the feed rate to increase the cuts per inch.

*Type of wood* — Generally, the harder the wood, the more power is required to plane it. Your planer may have sufficient power to make a $1/8$-inch-deep rough cut in soft pine while requiring you to reduce this to $1/16$ inch for harder woods such as walnut and cherry. For extremely hard woods like oak and maple, the maximum practical depth of cut may be only $1/32$ inch. The hardness of the wood also affects the feed rate — the harder the wood, the slower you should feed it.

*Wood grain* — Straight, clear grain is easiest to plane. You can take a deep cut at a high feed rate and produce a fairly smooth surface. Knots, burls, and figured wood grain, however, are much more difficult to cut. Not only do they require more power, they are prone to chipping and tearing. *(SEE FIGURE 2-17.)* To produce an acceptable surface, you must reduce the depth of cut and the feed rate. Also make sure the knives are sharp and free of pitch. **Note:** Highly figured wood may continue to chip no matter how shallow the cut or how slow the feed. When this is the case, plane the stock until it's slightly thicker than needed, then sand it to its final thickness.

**2-17  Figured wood doesn't have a** consistent grain direction; it presents both end grain and long grain on its surface. Because of this, it's difficult to plane. The planer knives tend to lift the end grain and tear it out, leaving the surface chipped and gouged. You can reduce the tearing by using a shallow depth of cut and a slow feed rate. Also make sure the knives are as clean and as sharp as possible. If you plane a lot of figured wood, you may want to reduce the cutting angle by having a face bevel ground on the knives, as shown on page 19. If none of these things helps, *sand* the stock to its final thickness. See page 95 for plans and instructions on how to make a thickness sander.

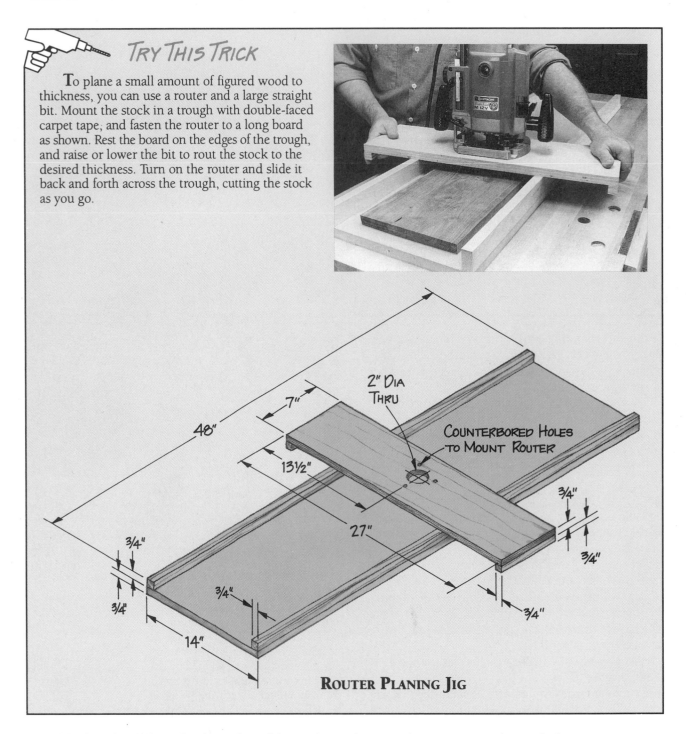

### TRY THIS TRICK

To plane a small amount of figured wood to thickness, you can use a router and a large straight bit. Mount the stock in a trough with double-faced carpet tape; and fasten the router to a long board as shown. Rest the board on the edges of the trough, and raise or lower the bit to rout the stock to the desired thickness. Turn on the router and slide it back and forth across the trough, cutting the stock as you go.

2" DIA THRU

COUNTERBORED HOLES TO MOUNT ROUTER

48"

7"

13½"

27"

¾"

¾"

¾"

¾"

¾"

¾"

14"

**ROUTER PLANING JIG**

*Width of stock* — The wider the surface of the stock, the more power is needed to plane it. If the wood is fairly narrow, you can take a deep cut at a high feed rate. But you may have to reduce the depth of cut and the feed rate to surface wide boards.

How do you know that you've set the depth of cut and the feed rate correctly? Judge by the results. If the planer is cutting a smooth surface without bogging

down, and you're getting the work done in a reasonable amount of time, the settings are okay.

Stand to one side of the planer as you work. Don't stand directly in front of the infeed opening; the wood may kick back. Feed the wood so the knives cut *downhill,* shaving the grain rather than digging into it. (*SEE FIGURE 2-18.*) Remove approximately the same amount of stock from both faces; otherwise, the board may cup.

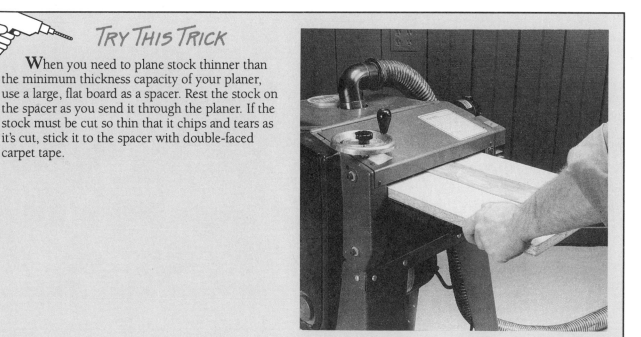

## TRY THIS TRICK

**W**hen you need to plane stock thinner than the minimum thickness capacity of your planer, use a large, flat board as a spacer. Rest the stock on the spacer as you send it through the planer. If the stock must be cut so thin that it chips and tears as it's cut, stick it to the spacer with double-faced carpet tape.

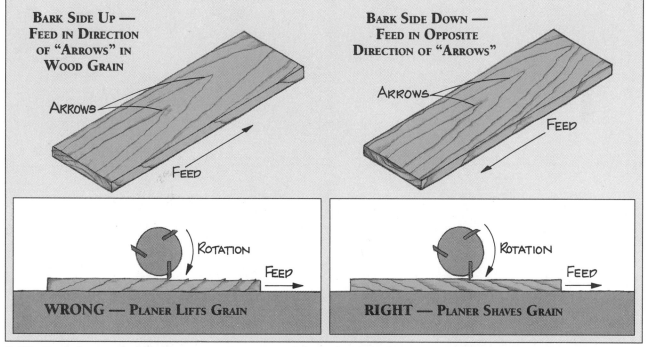

BARK SIDE UP — FEED IN DIRECTION OF "ARROWS" IN WOOD GRAIN

ARROWS

FEED

BARK SIDE DOWN — FEED IN OPPOSITE DIRECTION OF "ARROWS"

ARROWS

FEED

ROTATION

FEED

WRONG — PLANER LIFTS GRAIN

ROTATION

FEED

RIGHT — PLANER SHAVES GRAIN

**2-18 Feed the wood so the knives** cut *downhill,* cutting *with* the wood grain. If they cut against the grain, the wood will chip and tear. If you can, use the *grain arrows* in the face of the stock to help you decide which direction to feed a board. If the board is bark-side *up,* feed the wood *with* the arrows. If the bark side is *down,* feed the wood *against* the arrows. Oftentimes, especially when planing rough stock, it's difficult to tell which way to feed the stock just by inspecting it. Make a trial pass, watching and listening for problems. If the planer tears the wood grain, reverse the board end for end before the next pass. If the grain direction is inconsistent, the board will tear out no matter which way you feed it. In these instances, reduce the depth of cut and the feed rate to keep the torn grain to a minimum.

In addition to planing the faces of boards, you can also plane the edges. This will cut one edge of a board perfectly parallel. If you plane the edges of several boards without changing the thickness adjustment, the planer will cut them all to precisely the same width. (*SEE FIGURE 2-19.*) As when planing faces, the machine will not necessarily cut the edges straight or true. If you want the edges of a board to be straight *and* parallel, you must joint one edge before planing the other.

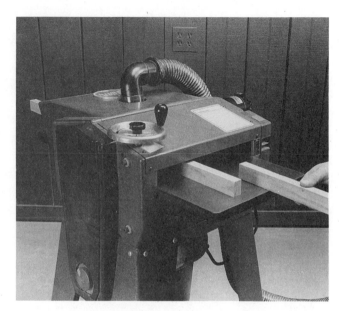

**2-19  To plane the edge of a board** safely, it must be stable when resting on its edge. If it's too thin or too wide, it may fall over in the planer and kick back. To avoid problems, follow this rule of thumb — don't edge-plane boards that are less than 1/2 inch wide or more than four times wider than they are thick.

## TRY THIS TRICK

In addition to cutting parallel surfaces, you can also use the planer to cut tapers. Rest the stock on a wedge-shaped spacer and send the stock through the planer low-end first so the knives don't dig into the grain. Adjust the depth of cut to plane the high end, then gradually reduce the thickness for subsequent passes until you've cut the complete taper.

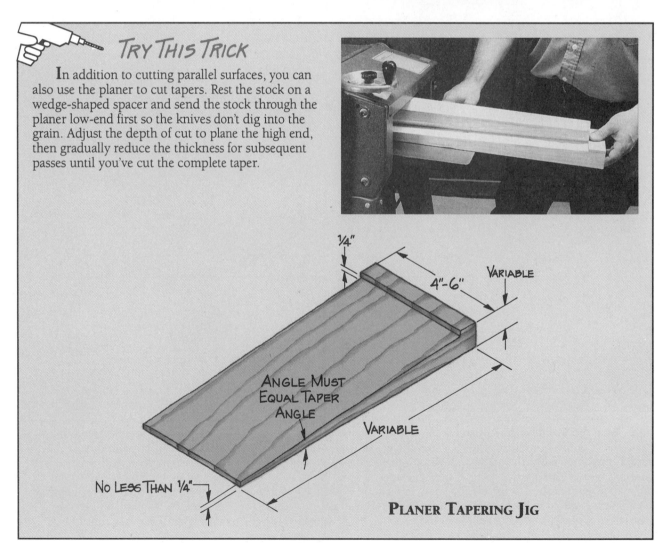

¼"

4"-6"

VARIABLE

ANGLE MUST EQUAL TAPER ANGLE

VARIABLE

NO LESS THAN ¼"

**PLANER TAPERING JIG**

# TROUBLESHOOTING THE PLANER

| PROBLEM | POSSIBLE CAUSE | SOLUTION |
| --- | --- | --- |
| Planer bogs down, trips circuit breaker. | Depth of cut is too deep or feed rate is too high. | Reduce depth of cut or feed rate. |
| Wood is difficult to feed or sticks in planer; planer leaves burn marks in surface. | Bed requires lubrication. <br> Feed roller pressure is too high. <br> Pressure bar is set too low. <br> Bed rollers are too low. | Wax and buff bed. <br> Reduce roller pressure. <br> Raise pressure bar. <br> Raise bed rollers. |
| Wood is pulled to one side as it feeds through planer. | Feed roller pressure is uneven. <br> Feed rollers are worn. | Adjust roller pressure. <br> Replace feed rollers. |
| Wood is not cut to same thickness from side to side. | Bed is not parallel to cutterhead. <br> Knives are not set properly. | Adjust bed parallel to cutterhead. <br> Reset knives. |
| Planer cuts a snipe in ends of board. | Feed roller pressure is too low. <br> Pressure bar is set too high. <br> Bed rollers are too high. <br> Long board is not properly supported. <br> Board is warped or crooked. | Increase roller pressure. <br> Lower pressure bar. <br> Lower bed rollers. <br> Support board with roller stand. <br> True board on jointer before planing. |
| Planer chips and tears wood grain. | Planer is cutting against grain. <br><br> Wood grain is figured. <br><br><br> Knives are dull. | Reverse board end for end, or reduce depth of cut or feed rate. <br> Reduce depth of cut or feed rate; sharpen the knives; sand or rout stock to final thickness. <br> Touch up or replace knives. |
| Planer leaves fuzzy surface. | Wood is not dry enough to plane. <br><br> Normal for basswood, elm, cottonwood, and soft maple. | Allow wood to air for several months before using. <br> Live with it. |
| Planer leaves raised grain. | Wood is not dry enough to plane. <br><br> Feed roller pressure is too high. <br> Depth of cut is too shallow for soft wood. | Allow wood to air for several months before using. <br> Reduce roller pressure. <br> Increase depth of cut. |
| Planer leaves evenly spaced marks. | Feed rate is too high. <br> One knife is set too high. <br> Infeed roller pressure is too high. | Reduce feed rate. <br> Reset knives. <br> Reduce infeed roller pressure. |
| Planer leaves unevenly spaced marks. | Feed roller pressure is too low. <br> Pressure bar is too high. <br> Cutterhead is out of balance from improperly sharpened knives. <br> Cutterhead bearings are worn. | Increase roller pressure. <br> Lower pressure bar. <br> Replace knives with match-ground set. <br> Replace bearings. |
| Planer leaves raised lines. | Planer knives are nicked. | Replace nicked knives with sharp ones. |
| Planer leaves small indentations in surface from shavings. | Wood shavings aren't properly evacuated from planer. <br><br> Wood is not dry enough, so shavings stick to surface. | Check that dust chute is not clogged and that shavings have not become impacted on the outfeed roller. <br> Allow wood to air dry for several months before using. |

## PLANER MAINTENANCE

To keep your planer in good working condition:

■ Keep the machine clean and free of wood chips; periodically, blow or brush the sawdust from the thickness adjusting mechanism.

■ Wax and buff the bed so the wood slides across it easily. You may also wax the bed rollers. However, be careful not to get wax on the feed rollers.

■ Touch up the knives with a slip stone from time to time, and keep them free of wood pitch.

■ Have the knives sharpened by a professional sharpening service when they grow dull. You'll know they need sharpening when they no longer leave a smooth surface, the planer bogs down or labors as it cuts, and the cutting edges reflect a thin line of light.

# HOW TO PROPERLY PREPARE WOOD

**H**ave you ever studied the work of master woodworkers and wondered how they got their joints to fit so perfectly? Chances are, it doesn't have as much to do with joinery technique as it does with *how they prepared the wood.* If you properly prepare each board so the surfaces are straight, true, and square to one another, it's much easier to cut tight, close-fitting joints.

Many inexperienced woodworkers purchase kiln-dried lumber, already planed on two or more surfaces, and bring it back to their shops thinking it's ready to use. It isn't. In fact, knowledgeable craftsmen consider lumber prepared in this fashion *unusable* for fine woodworking. Whenever you take a board out of one environment and put it in another — for example, when you move it from the lumberyard to your shop — it begins to move. Slight differences in temperature and humidity cause the wood to expand and contract until it reaches an equilibrium with its new home. It may also cup, warp, bow, or twist as it seeks a new balance.

If you attempt to work the wood before it stabilizes, it will be in motion when you cut the joints. The dovetails that you were so proud of on Monday may be nothing to crow about by Friday. You can avoid this problem by waiting two or three weeks for the wood to stabilize, but if it comes to rest with a cup or a crook, you may not be able to use it at all. Because the wood was surfaced at the lumberyard and is already cut to its final thickness, there will not be enough extra stock to remove even a minor defect.

How do you prepare commercially kiln-dried wood properly? First of all, purchase *rough* lumber — *don't* have it surfaced at the lumberyard, no mat-

ter how much time you think it will save you. Lumberyards may set out only surfaced stock in their bins, but most will sell rough wood if you request it. Take the wood back to your shop, stack it horizontally (if possible) with spaces between the boards, and let it *shop-dry* for two or three weeks to reach an equilibrium with its new environment.

Once the wood has stabilized, select the boards you want to use. Carefully plan how you will cut them to make the parts of your project. As you measure and mark each piece, leave yourself some extra stock, making the pieces 1 to 2 inches longer and about $\frac{1}{2}$ to 1 inch wider than their final dimensions. Then cut the boards up as you've marked them, roughing out the parts. Craftsmen sometimes refer to this as *busting down* the rough lumber. **Note:** Don't bust down the lumber into pieces smaller than you can joint or plane safely. If the project requires small parts, group these together on a section of a board and cut the section free.

Busting down relieves stresses in the wood. As the tree grows, it often buttresses itself against the wind or gravity. Drying the wood creates further stress as the outside of the wood loses its moisture and begins to shrink before the inside. These internal tensions remain until you release them by cutting the wood to size. As they are released, the wood moves again. But since you've cut the parts oversize, you can true them with some judicious jointing and planing.

(As with a jointer knife, a dull planer knife develops a rounded *land* on the edge. This land reflects light.) **Note:** Make sure that the sharpening service *match-grinds* the knives so they're all the same size and weight. Otherwise, the cutterhead may be thrown out of balance. This will cause the cutterhead bearings to wear prematurely.

Keep a second set of knives on hand so you can replace the dull knives with sharp ones one at a time. As on the jointer, you shouldn't take all the knives out of the cutterhead, releasing all the tension at once. And if you have two sets of knives, you can continue to use the planer while the dull knives are being sharpened.

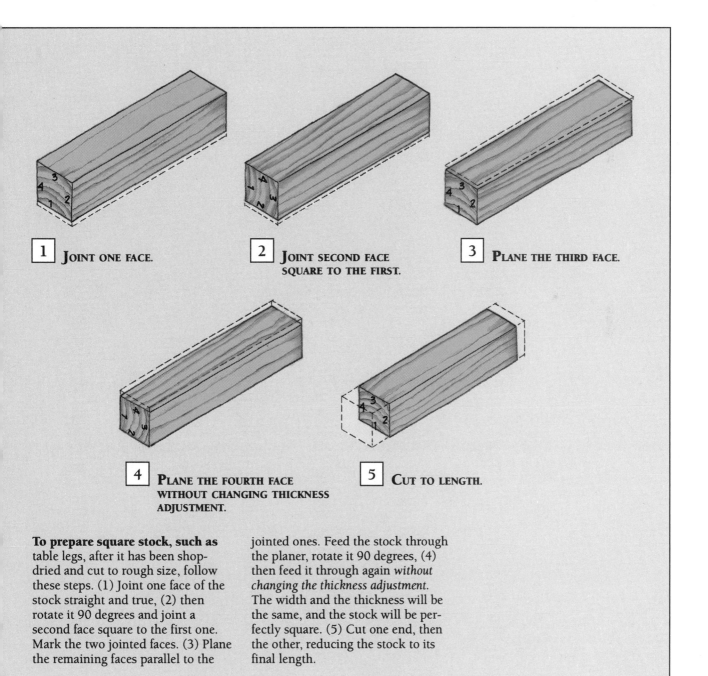

**1** JOINT ONE FACE.

**2** JOINT SECOND FACE SQUARE TO THE FIRST.

**3** PLANE THE THIRD FACE.

**4** PLANE THE FOURTH FACE WITHOUT CHANGING THICKNESS ADJUSTMENT.

**5** CUT TO LENGTH.

**To prepare square stock, such as** table legs, after it has been shop-dried and cut to rough size, follow these steps. (1) Joint one face of the stock straight and true, (2) then rotate it 90 degrees and joint a second face square to the first one. Mark the two jointed faces. (3) Plane the remaining faces parallel to the jointed ones. Feed the stock through the planer, rotate it 90 degrees, (4) then feed it through again *without changing the thickness adjustment.* The width and the thickness will be the same, and the stock will be perfectly square. (5) Cut one end, then the other, reducing the stock to its final length.

*(continued)* ▷

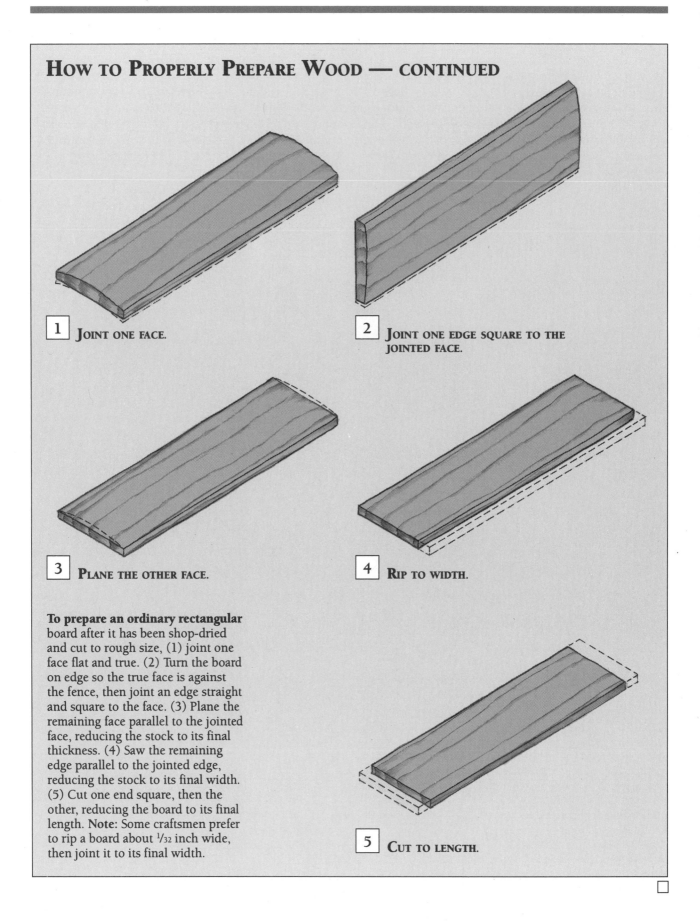

# HOW TO PROPERLY PREPARE WOOD — CONTINUED

**1** JOINT ONE FACE.

**2** JOINT ONE EDGE SQUARE TO THE JOINTED FACE.

**3** PLANE THE OTHER FACE.

**4** RIP TO WIDTH.

**5** CUT TO LENGTH.

**To prepare an ordinary rectangular** board after it has been shop-dried and cut to rough size, (1) joint one face flat and true. (2) Turn the board on edge so the true face is against the fence, then joint an edge straight and square to the face. (3) Plane the remaining face parallel to the jointed face, reducing the stock to its final thickness. (4) Saw the remaining edge parallel to the jointed edge, reducing the stock to its final width. (5) Cut one end square, then the other, reducing the board to its final length. **Note:** Some craftsmen prefer to rip a board about ¹/₃₂ inch wide, then joint it to its final width.

# 3

# SANDERS AND ABRASIVES

**W**hile jointers and planers shave boards smooth, sanders scrape them smooth with abrasives. Abrasives have always been part of woodworking, but sanders are a recent development. For thousands of years, craftsmen smoothed wooden surfaces with finely ground glass or brick dust, using blocks of cork or wood to rub the abrasive powder across the wood. Or, they polished the wood with patches of shark skin, another natural abrasive. It wasn't until the early nineteenth century, when strong, durable papers became available, that woodworkers began to glue abrasive powders to paper backing. This was originally known as *glasspaper,* since ground glass was the most commonly used abrasive.

Woodworkers quickly found that glasspaper could be mounted on discs and wound around drums to make mechanical abrasive tools. Ground glass, however, didn't hold up well in this new application; hard mineral *sands* such as garnet and aluminum oxide stayed sharp much longer. Consequently, abrasive power tools came to be called *sanders,* even though woodworkers continued to refer to paper-backed abrasives as glasspaper until well past the turn of the twentieth century. The term gradually died out, and was replaced with the more accurate *sandpaper.*

# ABRASIVES

Sandpaper is a scraping tool, consisting of abrasive sand adhered to a backing material with glue or resin. Each individual abrasive grain has sharp edges that scrape the wood surface, removing a small amount of stock. *(SEE FIGURE 3-1.)*

The smoothness and the quality of the sanded surface depends on the type of sandpaper used to scrape it. There are over a dozen different grades of paper commonly available at hardware stores, and more that can be purchased through mail-order suppliers. In addition, most grades can be found in different abrasives and mounted on various kinds and weights of backing material. To sort through all these possibilities and select the best sandpaper for a particular job, you must understand the choices.

## ABRASIVE MATERIALS

Four types of abrasive mineral sands are commonly used in woodworking *(SEE FIGURE 3-2)*:

*Flint* is the least expensive and the least durable. It's made from crushed quartz or silica and appears off-white or tan in color. Flint is not very hard and dulls quickly — even when new, it's not as sharp as other abrasives. Furthermore, it leaves flint dust imbedded in the wood grain, which may react chemically with some finishes. For these reasons, this mineral is *not* recommended for general sanding tasks or preparing a surface for a finish. However, because flint is inexpensive, it's useful for sanding resinous and gummy surfaces, and for removing wax, paint, and other finishes. It's cheap enough to treat like abrasive paper towels — when one sheet loads up, throw it away and get a fresh one.

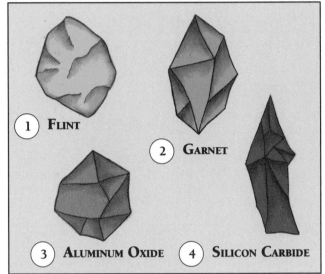

**3-2   If you inspect the four types** of woodworking abrasives under the microscope, the shape of the individual grains will tip you off as to what each one is used for. *Flint* (1) appears relatively dull; it won't cut as well or as quickly as the others. *Garnet* (2) is very sharp and cuts quickly and cleanly; it's preferred for hand sanding. *Aluminum oxide* (3) is also sharp, although the cutting edges aren't as pointed as garnet and they won't cut quite as cleanly. But the cutting edges are better buttressed — consequently, they last longer than garnet and are a better choice for machine sanding. *Silicon carbide* (4) is sharp and so pointed that the cutting edges snag on wood fibers and break off. Also, sanding dust packs between the pointed grains, loading the paper quickly. This makes silicon carbide better suited for sanding finishes instead of wood itself.

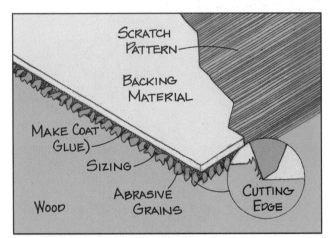

**3-1   Sandpaper is a scraping tool.** The sharp edges of the abrasive grains scrape the wood surface, removing a small amount of stock. As the grains do so, they level the rough and uneven spots in the wood surface, leaving a uniform *scratch pattern* — a series of tiny grooves dug by the grains. The smaller the grains, the finer the scratch pattern and the smoother the sanded surface appears to be.

*Garnet* varies in color from pink to reddish brown. It's preferred by most craftsmen for hand sanding because it's very sharp and it stays that way. This mineral is not particularly hard, but the garnet grains fracture as you use them, constantly creating fresh cutting edges. Because it stays sharp, garnet cuts quickly and produces an extremely smooth surface.

*Aluminum oxide* is a synthetic abrasive, made by fusing bauxite in an electric furnace. It is tan or brown in color. The cutting edges are very sharp when new, and even though they grow dull eventually, they are very durable and stand up to hard use. For this reason, aluminum oxide sandpaper is preferred for machine sanding.

*Silicon carbide* is the hardest and most expensive of the woodworking abrasives. It's also synthetic, made by heating silica and carbon to form a crystal. The color depends on its intended application — charcoal-colored silicon carbide sandpaper can be used for both wet and dry sanding, light gray is for dry sanding only. Although the abrasive is very hard, it's also very brittle and the cutting edges snap off easily when sanding unfinished wood. It's better suited for sanding finishes — either sanding between coats or rubbing out a final coat.

## ABRASIVE GRADES

The smoother you want to sand a wood surface, the finer the grade of abrasive you should use. Removing stock, surfacing, and grinding wood to shape all require fairly coarse grades. To true up wood joints, and level and smooth the surfaces, you need finer sandpaper. And to prepare stock for a finish and sand between coats of finish, you must use finer grades yet.

In addition, you often have to progress through several grades of paper to achieve the degree of smoothness you want. You can't just start sanding a rough surface with fine sandpaper and expect it to become smooth. Nor can you jump grades, starting with coarse paper and jumping to fine. (*See Figure 3-3.*) You must start and stop with the proper grades, working your way through the grades in between.

When commercial glasspaper first appeared, there were just four grades — flour, fine, middle, and strong. Today, there are not only more grades of sandpaper available, there are three ways to grade it — by name, grit number, and symbol.

The names — coarse, medium, fine, and so on — are the easiest to understand, but the least helpful when trying to decide what grades to use. The terms mean different things to different manufacturers — what one considers "very fine" sandpaper may be "extra fine" to another. The grit numbers and the symbols are much more accurate. Both of these designate the precise size of the abrasive grains.

Abrasive is sorted by sifting it through progressively finer sieves. Each sieve has a precise number of openings per linear inch. If an abrasive grain falls through a sieve with 80 openings per inch, but won't fall through the next-smaller sieve, it's labeled 80 grit. The corresponding symbol is 1/0 (one "aught"). Most manufacturers print both a name and either a grit number or a symbol on the backs of their abrasive products.

**3-3 As you sand, you must use** several consecutive grades of sandpaper, working your way from coarse to fine to achieve the degree of smoothness you want. Remember that the grains create a scratch pattern in the surface. The larger the grains (or the coarser the grade), the larger these scratches will be. When you move to the next-finer grade, you trade the first set of scratches for *slightly* smaller ones. If you jump grades, the fine abrasive grain may be too small to level the scratches without a lot of extra work — it will be like leveling a mountain with a garden spade. As a result, the wood surface will be left with an uneven scratch pattern, with deep scratches

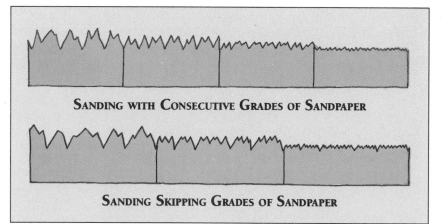

SANDING WITH CONSECUTIVE GRADES OF SANDPAPER

SANDING SKIPPING GRADES OF SANDPAPER

in among the fine ones. Because these deep scratches fill with fine sanding dust, they may be nearly invisible to you until you apply a finish to the wood. Then the finish

will darken the torn end-grain fibers in the deeper scratches, making them stand out from the surrounding wood. This will ruin the smooth, consistent appearance of the surface.

In most hardware stores, you can find a wide selection of abrasive grades, from 50 to 600 grit. You can purchase abrasives from 12 to 1200 grit through mail-order catalogs. And some automotive and aviation supply companies offer abrasive materials up to 12,000 grit. For most woodworking tasks, however, you won't need anything coarser or finer than you can find at a hardware store. To help choose the grade and type of abrasive you need, refer to "Abrasive Types, Grades, and Applications" below.

## OTHER ABRASIVE OPTIONS

In addition to abrasive materials and grades, there are several other options you should be aware of when selecting sandpaper.

*Backing Material* — The abrasive can be glued to either a cloth (usually a cotton and polyester blend) or a paper backing. Cloth is considerably more durable than paper, but it's also more expensive.

Cloth backing comes in two *weights*. "X" is the heavier of the two and is used mostly for machine sanding. Most sanding belts, for example, are made with X-weight cloth. "J" backings are lighter and more flexible. They can be used either for hand sanding or for light-duty machine sanding in which the abrasive must conform to shaped surfaces.

Paper backing comes in several weights, from "A" (the lightest) to "F" (the heaviest). Generally, the lighter papers are used for finer grits and the heavier papers for coarser grits. For most applications, "C" and "D" (sometimes referred to as *cabinet papers*) work best.

## ABRASIVE TYPES, GRADES, AND APPLICATIONS

| TYPES | | |
|---|---|---|
| **MATERIAL** | **COLOR** | **USES** |
| Flint | Off-white or tan | Removing wax, paint, and other finishing materials |
| Garnet | Pink or red-brown | Hand sanding |
| Aluminum Oxide | Tan or brown | Machine sanding |
| Silicon Carbide | Charcoal (wet/dry) or gray (dry only) | Sanding finishes |

| GRADES | | | |
|---|---|---|---|
| **NAME** | **GRIT NUMBERS** | **SYMBOLS** | **USES** |
| Extra Coarse | 12, 16, 20 | 4½, 4, 3½ | Grinding wood to shape |
| Very Coarse | 24, 30, 36 | 3, 2½, 2 | Grinding wood to shape, rough surfacing |
| Coarse | 40, 50 | 1½, 1 | Leveling surfaces removing stock, final surfacing |
| Medium | 60, 80, 100 | ½, 1/0, 2/0 | Smoothing surfaces, sanding joints flush |
| Fine | 120, 150, 180 | 3/0, 4/0, 5/0 | Preparing surfaces for "building" finishes such as varnish and polyurethane |
| Very Fine | 220, 240, 280 | 6/0, 7/0, 8/0 | Preparing surfaces or penetrating finishes such as tung oil and Danish oil |
| Extra Fine | 320, 360, 400 | 9/0, (none), 10/0 | Sanding finishes between coats |
| Ultra Fine | 500, 600, 1,000 | (none) | Sanding final finish |

## FOR YOUR INFORMATION

**H**ave you ever wondered why paper-backed abrasives curl up? For the same reason that a board will cup if you apply finish to only one face. The resin that adheres the abrasive to the paper acts like a coat of finish, creating a barrier to moisture. The uncoated side of the paper, however, absorbs and releases moisture easily. When the humidity changes, the fibers on the uncoated side shrink or swell, while the other side barely moves. This difference in movement causes the paper to curl.

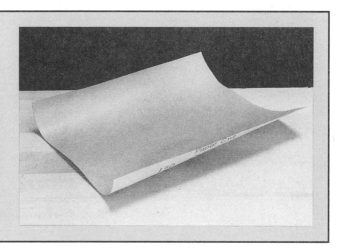

*Coating* — With the exception of flint, all abrasives are available in two different "coats." *(SEE FIGURE 3-4.)* *Open-coat* sandpapers have abrasives applied to just 50 to 70 percent of their surface. They are often used for sanding resinous woods or removing paint and finishes, since they don't load as easily. The open spaces between the abrasive grains allow the paper to clear itself more easily.

*Closed-coat* papers are covered completely with abrasives. Because there are more cutting surfaces per square inch, these papers cut faster than the open-coat variety. They are preferred for most sanding operations.

Besides open- and closed-coat papers, abrasives may also have *zinc stearate* coatings, a chemical treatment that prevents the sawdust from sticking to the sandpaper without interfering with the cutting action of the abrasive. Stearate-coated sandpaper doesn't load as fast and lasts longer than ordinary papers, especially when sanding softwoods or resinous hardwoods. The

coating turns the abrasive a dull white, and it is usually identified by words such as "no load," "no fill," and "non-clogging" on the paper backing.

**Note:** Zinc stearate may interfere with some finishes, in particular water-based acrylic finishes. The coating rubs off on the wood as you sand it and prevents the finish from adhering to the surface.

*Mounting* — Some abrasives are self-mounting so they can be attached quickly and easily to sanding blocks and machines. *(SEE FIGURE 3-5.)* The most common and least expensive mounting system is *pressure-sensitive adhesive,* or PSA. This adhesive is applied to the back of the sandpaper and protected with *release paper.* To mount a PSA-backed abrasive, peel off the release paper and press the sandpaper onto the block or pad. **Note:** PSA paper is temperature-sensitive. If the surface you want to stick it to is too cold, it may not stay. If you have trouble with PSA papers sticking in cool weather, warm the surfaces gently and evenly with a heat gun.

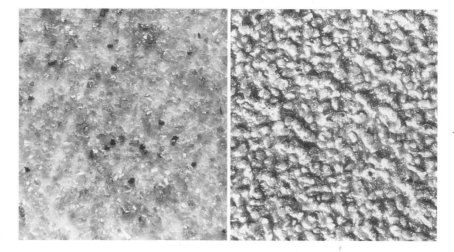

**3-4 Most abrasives come in both** *open* and *closed* coats. Closed-coat abrasives cover the backing material entirely, while open coats cover only 50 to 70 percent. The voids between the abrasive grains on open-coat materials keep the sawdust from loading the sandpaper when sanding resinous woods and removing finishes.

Other self-mounting abrasives use a *hook-and-loop* mounting system — the surface of the sanding block or pad has hundreds of tiny hooks that fasten to fiber loops on the back of the sandpaper. To mount the abrasive, just press the hooks and loops together. This system is more expensive than PSA, but changing abrasives is much easier. Furthermore, you can reuse hook-and-loop abrasives, mounting and remounting them many times, while you can only mount PSA abrasives once.

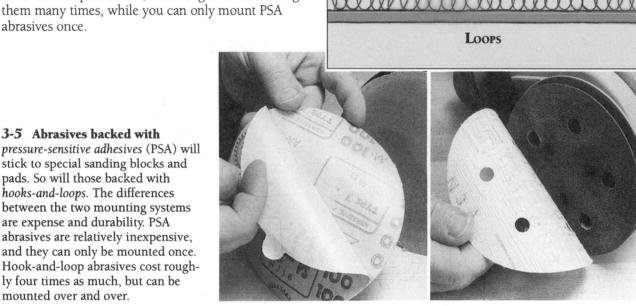

**3-5 Abrasives backed with** *pressure-sensitive adhesives* (PSA) will stick to special sanding blocks and pads. So will those backed with *hooks-and-loops*. The differences between the two mounting systems are expense and durability. PSA abrasives are relatively inexpensive, and they can only be mounted once. Hook-and-loop abrasives cost roughly four times as much, but can be mounted over and over.

# SANDING TOOLS

There is an amazing (and often bewildering) variety of sanding tools, machines, and accessories — abrasive blocks, pads, discs, drums, belts, and mops of all sizes and descriptions. No matter what the shape or size of the wooden surface you wish to sand, chances are that there's a tool somewhere that will sand it.

### STATIONARY SANDERS

Stationary and benchtop sanding tools can be divided into four categories:

*Stationary disc sanders* have the abrasive mounted on a spinning disc 6 to 20 inches in diameter. A small table in front of the disc supports the work while it's sanded. These sanders are useful for removing stock from flat and convex surfaces, sanding up to a mark or a line, fitting joints, and sanding wooden joints flush after they have been assembled. (*SEE FIGURES 3-6 AND 3-7.*)

On *stationary belt sanders,* the abrasive surface travels in a straight line, allowing you to sand with the grain. This makes belt sanders useful not only for removing stock, but also for surfacing and smoothing wood. These tools come in many sizes, from 1/2-inch-wide strip sanders to huge stroke sanders with a sanding surface as large and as wide as a door. (*SEE FIGURES 3-8 THROUGH 3-10.*)

*Drum sanders* are abrasive cylinders that revolve on shafts. Although most are power tool accessories, a few are mounted on their own motor and stand. Perhaps the most popular of these is the *oscillating drum sander,* which moves up and down as it spins. (*SEE FIGURE 3-11.*)

*Thickness sanders* reduce the thickness of the stock by abrading the surface. They are useful when you must surface figured stock, knots, thin boards, or end grain — boards that ordinary planer knives might chew up. Most are built along the same lines as a planer but have a large, horizontal abrasive drum instead of a cutterhead. (*SEE FIGURE 3-12.*) Refer to "Thickness Sander" on page 95 for plans and instructions on how to build one of these yourself.

**3-6 Disc sanders are often**
combined with other sanding
machines, particularly belt sanders
and strip sanders. A single motor
runs both abrasive tools. To use a
disc sander, rest the work you want
to sand on the work table and feed it
into the side of the disc that rotates
*down.* (If you use the side of the disc
that rotates up, it will lift the work
off the table.) On most machines,
the work table can be tilted so you
can sand accurate angles or true up
miter joints.

**3-7 While most disc sanders are**
flat, there are also *conical* discs. A
conical disc forms a very shallow
cone with a slope of no more than 2
or 3 degrees. This gives the sanding
surface a slight curve — when you
feed stock into the abrasive, it will
make contact along a narrow line
rather than contacting the entire
surface of the disc. With a fence to
guide the stock, you can sand boards
to width, and joint plywood and
figured wood.

**3-8 Mid-size stationary belt**
*sanders* mount belts between 4 and
6 inches wide, providing a generous
sanding surface. They're versatile

tools, capable of a wide range of
sanding tasks. Most can be used in
two positions — horizontally and
vertically. Sand concave surfaces

where the belt travels over the
rollers, and straight or convex surfaces where it rides over the flat
metal platen between the rollers.

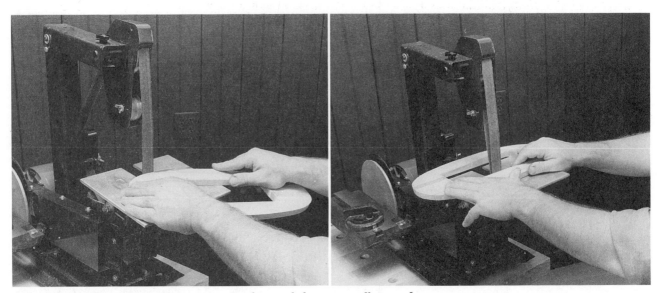

**3-9  Strip sanders use narrow** belts, just 1 or 2 inches wide, which travel vertically. A table supports the work as you press it against the belt. These tools are commonly used for sanding and shaping small parts, fitting joints, and sharpening. A few can be configured to sand the edges of interior cuts.

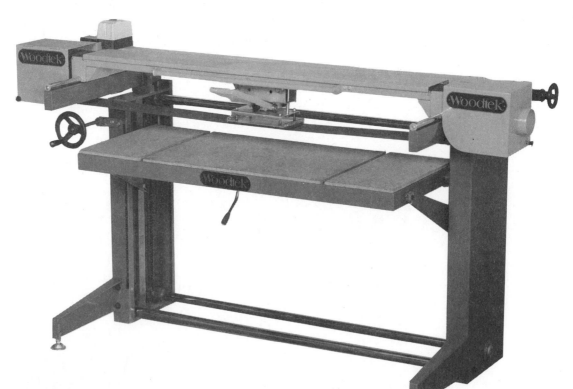

**3-10  Stroke sanders are among** the largest sanding machines, mounting belts up to 50 inches wide and over 12 feet long. The belt travels horizontally as you press it down against the surface of the stock with a large pad or *stroker*. This is a production tool, used for sanding large surfaces such as cabinet sides and doors. *Photo courtesy of Woodworker's Supply, Inc.*

**3-11  The abrasive cylinder on an** *oscillating drum sander* travels up and down slowly as it spins. There are two advantages to this dual motion. First, you can use more of the drum to sand the stock; consequently, the abrasive sleeve cuts faster and lasts longer. Second, the dual motion produces a much smoother surface. *Photo courtesy of Vega Enterprises, Inc.*

**3-12  A** *thickness sander* **uses a** long horizontal abrasive drum to reduce the thickness of the stock. Most of these are massive machines, too large and costly for the typical small shop. But the sander shown — the Performax S/T — is an abrasive thicknessing accessory that attaches to the arm of a radial arm saw. Performax also makes a benchtop model, the 16-32. Both machines can also be used to smooth large panels or glued-up stock, like a stroke sander. They cost much less than a stationary thickness sander, and you can store them out of the way when they're not needed. *Photo courtesy of Performax Products, Inc.*

## PORTABLE SANDERS

There are three types of portable sanding machines:

*Portable disc sanders* spin semi-flexible abrasive discs between 4 and 7 inches in diameter. A *sander/polisher* uses a simple circular motion for quick stock removal, grinding wood to shape, and polishing finishes. *(See Figure 3-13.)* A *random-orbit sander* has a mechanism that causes its disc to jig and jog unpredictably as it spins. This random motion produces a much smoother surface than a sander/polisher and makes the random-orbit sander suitable for both rough and finish sanding. *(See Figure 3-14.)*

*Portable belt sanders* are small, hand-held versions of stationary belt sanders. In fact, some manufacturers offer benchtop stands for their machines so you can use them as either a portable or a stationary tool. *(See Figures 3-15 and 3-16.)* Like their stationary cousins, they are very versatile, performing almost all major sanding tasks well.

*Pad sanders* are the smallest and lightest power sanders — often small enough to be held comfortably in one hand. The cheaper machines vibrate; better ones oscillate or *orbit* between 10,000 and 20,000 times a minute to create a smooth surface. There are two types of pad sanders — sheet sanders or *palm sanders,* which mount from one sixth to one half sheet of standard-size sandpaper, and detail sanders, which

have small, triangular pads to reach into corners and crevices. (*SEE FIGURES 3-17 AND 3-18.*) All are used almost exclusively for finish sanding — they won't remove stock fast enough to do anything else.

**3-13** A *sander/polisher* **spins an** abrasive disc in a simple circular motion. Although it can be used to quickly remove stock, it's not recommended for finish sanding because the disc leaves swirl marks in the wood. Paradoxically, the machine works well for rubbing out and polishing a finish. Cover the disc with a cloth *bonnet,* then use the bonnet to apply rubbing compound or another extremely fine abrasive to the cured finish. **Note:** Don't mistake a *disc grinder* for a sander/polisher. The two machines look similar, but sander/polishers are low-speed tools, turning at 2,000 to 3,000 rpm. Grinders revolve at 5,000 rpm or faster — much too fast for sanding and polishing.

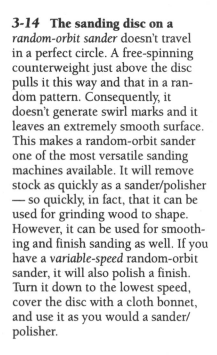

**3-14** **The sanding disc on a** *random-orbit sander* doesn't travel in a perfect circle. A free-spinning counterweight just above the disc pulls it this way and that in a random pattern. Consequently, it doesn't generate swirl marks and it leaves an extremely smooth surface. This makes a random-orbit sander one of the most versatile sanding machines available. It will remove stock as quickly as a sander/polisher — so quickly, in fact, that it can be used for grinding wood to shape. However, it can be used for smoothing and finish sanding as well. If you have a *variable-speed* random-orbit sander, it will also polish a finish. Turn it down to the lowest speed, cover the disc with a cloth bonnet, and use it as you would a sander/polisher.

**3-15  This portable belt sander** can also be used as a stationary belt sander with a special benchtop stand accessory. The stand holds the sander in both a horizontal and a vertical position. As a portable tool, the sander is used mostly for sanding large surfaces. With the optional stand, it can also be used for small work.

**3-16  If you use a portable belt** sander for smoothing and finish sanding, a *sanding frame* is a good investment. This frame limits how much stock the belt sander can remove at one time, and it helps keep the tool from gouging the stock or creating low spots.

**3-17  The larger of these two** *pad sanders* mounts a third sheet of sandpaper, while the smaller one mounts a quarter sheet. There are also sanders which mount one sixth and one half sheets. Larger sanders get the job done faster because they have more sanding surface. Smaller ones are easier to maneuver because they're lighter and can be held in one hand. All sizes are used for finish sanding.

**3-18  A *detail sander* is designed** to reach those areas you can't get to with a palm sander. The small, triangular pad will reach into corners and shallow crevices without marring the surrounding surfaces.

## SANDING ACCESSORIES

You can also purchase sanding accessories that mount on drill presses, lathes, portable drills, flexible-shaft machines, and other tools with either a chuck or a power take-off.

*Drum sanders* come in dozens of sizes and will sand concave surfaces, the surfaces of interior cuts, and edges of all descriptions. (*SEE FIGURES 3-19 AND 3-20.*) *Contour sanders* — abrasive mops, flap sanders, and flutter sheets — are designed to sand three-dimensional surfaces. These have flexible abrasive fingers attached to a spinning shaft or disc. As you hold the wood against the revolving sander, the fingers conform to the shape of the surface and reach into cracks and crevices. (*SEE FIGURE 3-21.*)

**3-20  Most drum sanders are** made of solid rubber and are covered with a stiff paper-backed abrasive sleeve. *Pneumatic drum sanders,* however, are inflatable and are covered with a flexible, cloth-backed *pump sleeve.* By pumping more air into the drum or letting some out, you can adjust the firmness of the sanding surface. By changing the air pressure so the drum is fairly soft, you can sand rounded and contoured surfaces.

**3-19  *Drum sander* accessories are** commonly available in sizes from $1/4$ inch to 8 inches in diameter. Most have a shaft protruding from one end so they can be mounted in a drill chuck. Larger units sometimes have a socket that slips over a motor arbor.

## HAND SANDING TOOLS

When hand sanding, it helps to back up the abrasive with something rigid that conforms to the surface you're smoothing. Otherwise, it's very difficult to sand the surface evenly. Without a stiff *sanding block,* you may round over corners, create low spots, or otherwise change the shape of the wood. However, this block must not be too stiff. If it doesn't have some give, the abrasive won't cut as well or last as long.

Most hand sanding tools are sanding blocks of one kind or another. Commercial blocks come in all shapes and sizes — flat, pointed, concave, and convex. They can be made from many different materials — wood, leather, plastic, felt, and rubber. Some have special devices for holding the abrasive paper; others are self-loading, with built-in rolls of abrasives. (*SEE FIGURE 3-22.*)

**3-21 Contour sanders, such as** abrasive mops, flap sanders, and flutter sheets, are flexible abrasives that conform to the surface you're sanding. All of these are power tool accessories that can be mounted in a chuck or on a motor shaft.

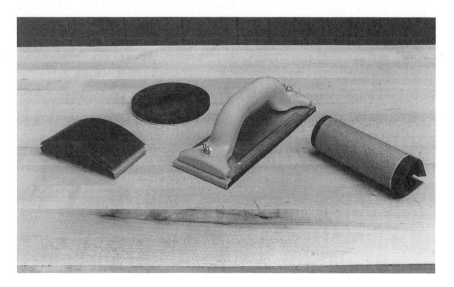

**3-22 Most commercial hand** sanding tools are *sanding blocks.* These come in all sizes, shapes, and designs, and there are more being introduced all the time.

**K**eep an old hacksaw blade around to help cut sandpaper to fit your sanding blocks. Press the blade down against the sheet with one hand; pull up on the sheet with the other hand. The teeth of the blade will separate the paper quickly and cleanly.

There are many other materials that you can use to back up abrasives for hand sanding. Wrap sandpaper around cotton balls, steel wool, or a sponge to make a sanding pad that will conform to contoured surfaces. An ordinary chalkboard eraser makes an excellent sanding block for flat surfaces. You can also use it to apply pumice, rottenstone, and other fine abrasives when rubbing out a finish.

Or, you can make your own sanding blocks. Take a scrap of wood small enough to fit your hand, cut it to the shape you need, and cover the *bearing* surface — the surface that will bear against the wood as you sand — with felt or cork. Glue this material in place with white or yellow wood glue. You might also cover

the bearing surface with leather or rubber gasket material (available at most hardware stores), affixing it with contact cement or silicone caulk. The advantage of leather and rubber is that PSA sandpapers will stick to them. (*SEE FIGURES 3-23 AND 3-24.*)

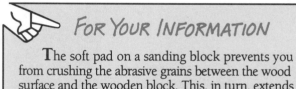

**T**he soft pad on a sanding block prevents you from crushing the abrasive grains between the wood surface and the wooden block. This, in turn, extends the life of the sandpaper.

**T**o make a disposable sanding block that conforms to the surface you want to sand, cut a block of rigid foam insulation with a coping saw to fit the surface. Fold or bend the sandpaper to fit the block.

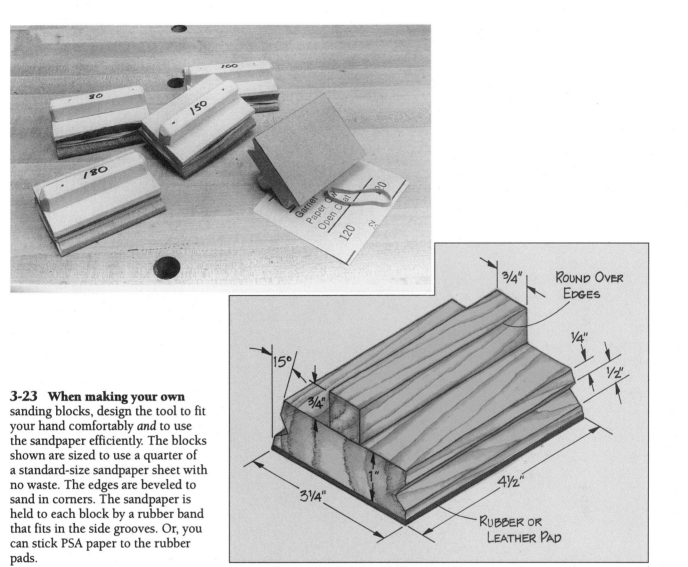

**3-23 When making your own**
sanding blocks, design the tool to fit
your hand comfortably *and* to use
the sandpaper efficiently. The blocks
shown are sized to use a quarter of
a standard-size sandpaper sheet with
no waste. The edges are beveled to
sand in corners. The sandpaper is
held to each block by a rubber band
that fits in the side grooves. Or, you
can stick PSA paper to the rubber
pads.

**3-24 You may also want to make**
sanding sticks to fit odd surfaces.
The most frequently used shapes are
round, square, and triangular. Cover
the bearing surfaces of these sticks
with felt, leather, or rubber, just as
you do when making sanding blocks.

# 4

# SANDING TECHNIQUES

Sanding includes an amazing variety of woodworking tasks. You're sanding when you use a 40-grit abrasive disc to scoop out the seat of a Windsor chair. You're also sanding when you give that same chair a final rubdown with a palm sander and 220-grit sandpaper to prepare it for a tung oil finish. You're sanding when you grind away the old paint from the side of your house with a disc sander and 50-grit paper, just as you are when you level a coat of lacquer on a refinished family heirloom with a sanding block and 400-grit paper.

What all of these activities have in common is that you are using an abrasive to scrape away a *controlled* amount of material from a surface. In each case, you want to sand the surface *flat* (without noticeable high or low spots), or — if the surface is contoured — *fair* (without awkward or unsightly transitions in the surface curves). And you want to leave the surface *smoother* than when you began. Remember all three of these criteria no matter what sanding task you engage in. Too often craftsmen concentrate on just one or two, and end up having to do more work than necessary.

# CHOOSING THE TOOLS AND THE MATERIALS

The first step is to choose the sanding tools and abrasives you will use. You'll rarely use just one tool or abrasive; most tasks require a combination of tools and several grades or types of abrasives.

## SELECTING SANDING TOOLS

Ask yourself: Should you use power sanders, or sand by hand? What machines should you use? What hand sanding aids? If you use more than one, when do you make the transition? There are some simple, common-sense rules of thumb to determine what tool to use and when.

**4-1 Stationary power sanders** and accessories are the best choice for precision sanding. Work tables, miter gauges, and fences guide the stock and increase your control. Here, a drum sanding accessory is being used to sand up to a line. The work table supports the work, keeping it square to the drum and allowing the craftsman to concentrate on the line.

**4-2 Sanding tools differ markedly** in their ability to remove stock. Here are three portable sanding tools that were equipped with the same coarse abrasive and used to sand a board for five minutes. The belt sander has almost cut clear through the stock, the random-orbit sander has created a large gouge, and the pad sander has barely made a slight depression.

When sanding pieces that are small enough to hold comfortably, and you wish to remove stock quickly, use a stationary power sander. For example, you might sand the flat surfaces of a toy on a stationary belt sander. You should also use stationary sanders when you need to do precision sanding, as when truing up a compound miter joint. (*SEE FIGURE 4-1.*)

When sanding objects that are too large to hold, if you wish to remove stock quickly, use a portable machine such as a portable belt sander, random-orbit sander, or sander/polisher. You might, for example, choose one of these to sand the pins and tails of a dovetail joint flush on an assembled blanket chest. If you want to remove stock more slowly, use a pad sander. (*SEE FIGURE 4-2.*)

When finesse and control are paramount, and you must remove stock slowly, sand by hand. It's very risky to use power sanders when you want to preserve a crisp edge or avoid sanding through a thin veneer covering. Even a pad sander may not give you enough control in these circumstances. You will also have to rely on hand sanding techniques to smooth areas or shapes that you cannot reach with a machine.

You don't need a large selection of power sanders and hand sanding aids to perform a wide variety of sanding chores, but you do need more than one or two if time is important. Well-equipped craftsmen and small shops rely, for the most part, on seven machines and accessories — a stationary disc sander, portable or stationary belt sander, strip sander, drum sander, contour sander, random-orbit sander, and pad sander — plus an assortment of sanding blocks. The combined capabilities of these tools allow you to tackle any sanding job, small or large, and accomplish it in a reasonable length of time.

## SELECTING ABRASIVES

It's just as important to work with the right abrasives as it is to work with the right tools. If you begin sanding with a grit that's too coarse, you may remove more stock than you want to. If you start with one that's too fine, the task may take you too much time. The type of abrasive material — garnet, aluminum oxide, silicon carbide — is important too. If you sand with the wrong abrasive, you can waste time and material, and the results may not be what you were hoping for.

The chart "Abrasive Types, Grades, and Applications" on page 44 will help you choose the appropriate abrasive materials and grades you need for a particular sanding job. Also be aware that every sanding tool is designed to work best with a specific *range* of abrasive grades. If you use a grade that's too coarse or too fine for the tool, once again, you may not get good results. Here's a list of abrasive ranges for most popular sanding tools:

- Belt sander (portable) — 60 to 120 grit
- Belt sander (stationary) — 36 to 120 grit
- Contour sander — 60 to 220 grit
- Disc sander — 12 to 120 grit
- Drum sander (hard) — 60 to 150 grit
- Drum sander (pneumatic) — 60 to 220 grit
- Pad sander — 100 to 320 grit
- Random-orbit sander — 80 to 320 grit

- Sander/polisher — 36 to 1000 grit
- Strip sander — 36 to 150 grit
- Thickness sander — 12 to 60 grit

The numbers on this list aren't cast in concrete, of course. There are some exceptions for *specific* sanding techniques. But for general sanding chores, these ranges present useful guidelines. They also show what tasks each tool is designed to do, and help to identify sanding problems that you might encounter. For example, if you didn't already know that a pad sander was intended for finish sanding, you might guess from its 100- to 320-grit range. Or, if the abrasive belt on a strip sander is loading quickly, it may be because you are using a fine grade that was intended for sharpening rather than sanding. *(SEE FIGURE 4-3.)*

When selecting abrasives, also pay attention to the coat and the backing material. Use a closed coat when using a pad sander or sanding by hand — this will increase the cutting action. Use an open coat with other power sanders and accessories to keep the abrasive from loading or clogging. Use paper backing for light sanding tasks and for machines in which the abrasive is mounted solidly on a pad, disc, or hard drum. Use cloth backing for more demanding chores and for sanders that require running belts or flexible sleeves.

**4-3  What happens if you use a** coarser abrasive grade than the tool was designed to handle? Usually, the machine won't have enough sanding area or power to make good use of the coarse grit. In the photo on the left, for example, a pad sander was loaded with 50-grit paper and used for several minutes to sand a hard maple surface. The surface has been roughened, but very little stock has been removed. And if you use a grade finer than the usual range, the paper often loads and the wood burns. This is what happened when the strip sander on the right was used to sand wood with a 320-grit sharpening belt.

# COMMON SANDING PROCEDURES

These tips will speed your sanding chores and help produce better results.

### FOR GENERAL SANDING

■ Make sure the dust collectors on your sanders are hooked up and working, and wear a dust mask as you work. Sanding dust can be a health hazard. Refer to "Sanding Safely" on page 65 for more information.

■ Clean the wood with a brush or shop vacuum before you start, and wipe the dust off frequently as you sand. This keeps the sandpaper from clogging with dirt and sawdust, makes it easier to locate blemishes and raised areas that require additional sanding, and helps you see the scratch pattern as it develops.

■ Remove any hardened glue beads with a glue scraper. (SEE FIGURE 4-4.) Don't try to sand them off; the glue will load the sandpaper.

■ Place the object you're sanding on an old towel or a rubber mat. Whenever you switch grits or change sandpaper, shake out the towel or brush off the mat. This will help prevent the piece from becoming dented or scratched.

**4-4 Most wood glues are** *thermoplastic* — when you heat them they become a gooey liquid. If you try to sand glue beads off a surface, the friction from sanding heats the glue and liquifies it. The liquid glue sticks to the sandpaper, solidifies as it cools, and clogs the abrasive. Sandpaper will stay sharper and last longer if you remove all excess glue with a *glue scraper* before you start sanding.

### TRY THIS TRICK

**F**or an excellent sanding mat, try the rubberized, open-weave fabric sold in carpet stores to keep throw rugs from sliding around on slick floors. The fabric not only protects the wood from becoming dented and scratched, but also keeps it from sliding around your workbench.

■ Shine a bright light across the wood surface at an angle as you sand to help spot minute imperfections. (SEE FIGURE 4-5.)

■ Don't sand out dents. These can be raised simply by steaming the dented area with a steam iron. (SEE FIGURE 4-6.)

■ Sand at an *angle* to the wood grain to remove stock quickly. However, when you smooth the surface or prepare it for a finish, sand *with* the grain as much as possible. When you sand at an angle to the grain, the abrasive travels across the long wood cells and tears them. The surface looks ragged and fuzzy. Sanding with the grain combs the cells. There is less tearing, and the surface appears smoother.

■ Don't press too hard as you sand. If you press the sander down, it will cut more quickly for a few moments, but the abrasive will rapidly clog with sanding dust and will soon become ineffective. *All* sanding tools, from sanding blocks to stroke sanders, cut faster, longer, and smoother if you keep the pressure light. Some sanding tools will bog down if you press too hard, and this may damage the motor. Random-orbit sanders will stop completely.

■ Don't set sander speeds too high, or the resulting friction will heat the wood and burn it.

■ Keep the sander (or the object) moving. If you let the sander dwell on any one spot for too long, it

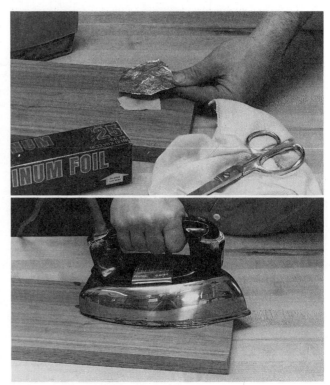

**4-5  When you sand wood to**
smooth the surface or prepare it for
a finish, you must remove the *minute*
imperfections — slightly raised areas,
small steps between glued-up boards,
raised lines left by planer or jointer
knives, mill marks, and scratches.
All of these are difficult to see using
only overhead lighting. Instead,
shine a bright light across the project
at a steep angle. In this oblique light,
the surface flaws will cast shadows
that are many times larger than the
flaws themselves. When there are no
more shadows, you know the surface
is smooth.

**4-6  To raise a dent, wet a small**
piece of paper towel and place it
over the dented area. Cover the
towel with a piece of aluminum foil,
and apply a hot steam iron (with the
steam *off*) to the foil for several
seconds. The iron turns the water in
the towel to steam, and the foil keeps
it from escaping into the air. The
steam penetrates the wood, causing
the compressed fibers in the dent to
expand, and the dent disappears.
**Note:** Be careful not to hold the iron
in place so long that it scorches the
wood.

may remove too much stock, creating a low spot in
the surface. Additionally, the constant friction may
heat the wood to the point that it scorches.

■ Mask off any areas that you don't want to sand.
Use masking tape when sanding by hand or with a
pad sander; cover the area with scrap wood when
using more aggressive sanding tools. (*SEE FIGURE 4-7.*)

■ If the sandpaper loads too fast, switch to a coarser
grit. You may be using an abrasive grade that's too fine
for the job. Or, the surface may not yet be smooth
enough to sand with a fine grit — work your way up
to it.

■ Don't skip grades of sandpaper, or change grades
too soon. Sand until the surface looks smooth and
uniform under a bright light. This indicates that the
scratch pattern is fairly even and that the surface is
ready for a finer grade.

■ Sand each surface of the project in turn, following a consistent pattern. Repeat the pattern every time
you change grades of sandpaper. You'll be less likely
to forget a surface.

■ Sand each surface of the project evenly, removing
the same amount of stock from all areas. It's okay to
dwell on problem areas when you first start to sand a

project. But once you've worked your way past the first or second abrasive grades, the problems should be gone.

■ If you've worked your way up to fine grades of abrasive and find a high spot you've missed, you can usually sand it without changing back to a coarser grade. However, if you discover a scratch or a blemish, drop back to a coarser grade and sand just that area. Work your way back up to the fine grade you were using when you discovered the imperfection.

■ When you're preparing a surface to receive a finish, wet the surface with a damp rag after you've sanded it with the finest grade. Although this will raise the grain slightly, the water will not hurt the wood. Instead, it restores crushed wood fibers and makes any loose fibers — called *whiskers* — stand up. Let the surface dry completely, then sand once more with the finest grade, smoothing the raised grain and knocking off the whiskers.

## FOR STATIONARY SANDERS

■ Use a work table, fence, or miter gauge to support the work whenever possible. This practice is safer, and it also helps you to be precise in your sanding.

■ Adjust the distance between the abrasive and the work table until it is as small as possible — no more than ⅛ inch. (*SEE FIGURE 4-8.*) This reduces the risk that your fingers will be pinched in the machine.

■ Always sand on the *down* side of a disc or belt. (*SEE FIGURE 4-9.*) Use the movement of the abrasive to help hold the work on the work table.

■ In addition to using a work table, fence, or miter gauge to guide the stock, you can also make a variety of simple jigs for precision sanding. For plans on how to make these accessories, see "Precision Sanding Jigs" on page 69.

■ When using a disc sander, you can control the amount of abrasive you remove by working with different areas of the disc. Near the outside of the disc,

**4-7 Sometimes the only way to** prevent yourself from sanding crossgrain on certain areas of a project is to cover those areas with masking tape or scrap wood. If you use wood, clamp it to the surface or stick it in place with double-faced carpet tape. You can also use this technique to preserve crisp lines and edges.

**4-8 Adjust the worktable to** within ⅛ inch of the abrasive. Where the belt or disc travels past the work table, there is a *pinch point*. If you should let your fingers stray too close to the moving abrasive, they may be dragged into this opening and pinched — or worse. Even though sanders have no knives or cutters, large abrasive machines can tear off or sand away fingers if you give them the chance. By placing the work table close to the abrasive, you reduce the pinch point and decrease the risk that your hands might be caught in it.

the abrasive is traveling faster and will remove stock quickly. As you approach the center, the abrasive travels more slowly and doesn't remove stock as rapidly.

■ If you need to sand small parts, attach them to push sticks or push blocks with carpet tape. (*SEE FIGURE 4-10.*) This will let you sand them without removing your fingernails — or your fingers.

■ When you must sand the edges of several identical parts, stack them face to face and stick them together with double-faced carpet tape. Sand all the parts together, then take them apart and discard the tape. This is sometimes referred to as *pad sanding*.

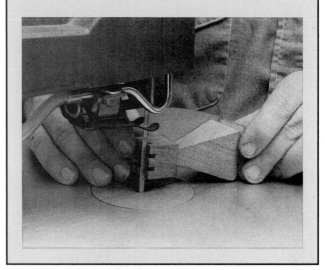

## TRY THIS TRICK

**T**o sand small parts or parts with intricate shapes, wrap abrasive backed with pressure-sensitive adhesive (PSA) around the blade of a scroll saw or jig saw. Use the abrasive-covered saw like a miniature strip sander.

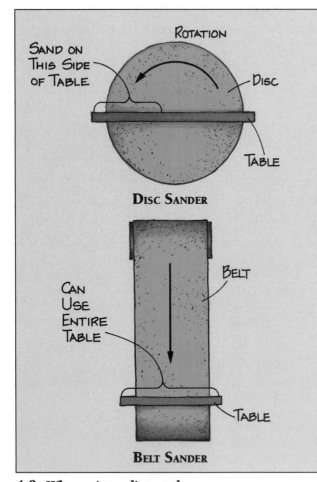

**4-9   When using a disc sander,** always sand on the *down* side of the disc — the half that is rotating down toward the table. When using a belt sander, set up the work table so the belt travels *down,* past the table. The motion of the abrasive helps hold the stock on the table, making the operation both safer and more accurate.

**4-10   Small parts may bring your** fingers uncomfortably close to the moving abrasives — and to dangerous pinch points. To sand these parts safely, attach them to a push stick, push block, or large wood scrap with double-faced carpet tape. Use the safety tool or the scrap to maneuver the part as you sand it.

## FOR PORTABLE SANDERS

■ Use the entire pad or disc when you sand; don't tip the sander on its edge. The sander cuts faster and more evenly if you use all the abrasive surface available to you. If you use just the edge, this area will wear out long before the rest of the abrasive.

■ Be careful not to let the sander rock when it overhangs an edge. (SEE FIGURE 4-11.) This will round the corners and arrises.

**TRY THIS TRICK**

To keep from accidentally sanding the power cord when using a portable sander, drape the cord over your shoulder.

## FOR HAND SANDING

■ Whenever possible, use a sanding block to back up the sandpaper — it's almost impossible to sand the surface level or fair without one.

■ Like portable sanders, sanding blocks may rock as you sand the perimeter of a surface, rounding over the edges. To prevent this, keep the blocks level.

■ When you can't use sanding blocks, cut the sandpaper sheets in quarters, then fold the quarter sheets in thirds. (SEE FIGURE 4-12.) This arrangement makes it easy to hold the sandpaper and lets you use all of the abrasive surface.

■ To sand in hard-to-reach cracks and crevices, use abrasive cords. (SEE FIGURE 4-13.)

■ Sand a lathe turning by hand with the turning mounted on the lathe. Remove the tool rest, turn the lathe on at medium speed, and hold the sandpaper against the spinning surface. (SEE FIGURE 4-14.)

■ Clean the surface of the sandpaper often by tapping it on the workbench. This will help clear the sanding dust and prevent the paper from loading as quickly.

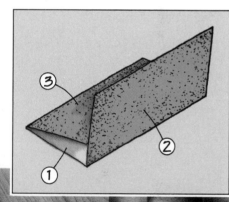

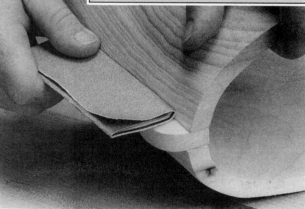

**4-12  When you're using just your** hands to back up a piece of sandpaper, fold the sheet in thirds, as shown, creating three abrasive surfaces. Use surface 1 until it's dull, then turn it over and use surface 2. When that's dull, tuck surface 2 under surface 3, and use that. This allows you to use the entire sheet without wasting any of it.

PAD SANDER ROCKS, ROUNDS EDGE

BACK UP EDGE WITH SCRAP

**4-11  The sander has a tendency** to tilt or rock when you sand close to the edges of a board. This will round over the edges, and can be prevented by keeping the tool level. In some cases, you may wish to back up the edges with scraps of wood to keep them crisp and square.

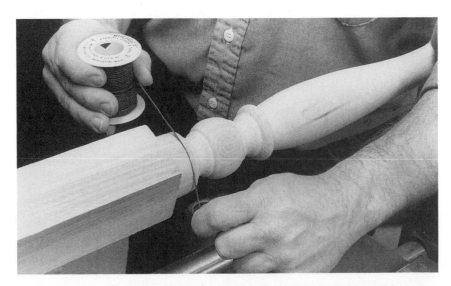

**4-13 Abrasive cords are designed** to reach areas that you can't get to with ordinary sandpaper. Simply cut off a length of cord, hold it in both hands, and work it back and forth across the surface.

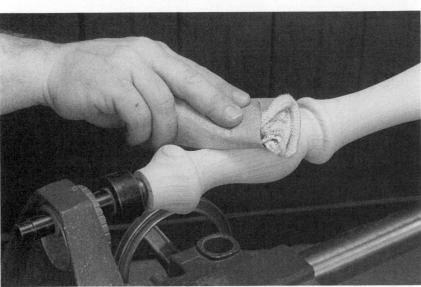

**4-14 When sanding a lathe** turning on the lathe, the friction often heats the sandpaper and makes it uncomfortable to hold. To protect your hands from this heat, wrap the sandpaper around a cloth pad or a sponge.

**4-15 When sandpaper loads up** with sawdust, clean it with a rubber abrasive cleaner, as shown. The rubber digs in between the grains and pops out impacted dust. It does *not,* however, sharpen a dull abrasive — you cannot restore a worn disc or belt simply by cleaning it. If a clean abrasive cuts slowly and tends to burn the wood, it's probably dull. Replace the abrasive; don't continue to clean it.

# SANDER MAINTENANCE

## CLEANING

Sanders require more maintenance than most wood-working tools for the simple reason that they generate more dust. As explained in "Sanding Safely" below, this fine dust is a mild abrasive that will eventually ruin bearings, rotors, and other moving parts. Because of this, it's important that you keep your sanders *clean*.

■ Make it a habit to vacuum a sander immediately after using it. This will help keep the fine dust from working its way into the bowels of the machine.

■ If any part of the sander becomes difficult to operate, it probably needs cleaning. For example, if you find it hard to turn a belt-tracking adjustment, or an on/off switch begins to stick, it's likely that the moving parts are clogged with sanding dust. Unplug the machine. Then, following the instructions in the owner's manual, take the machine apart and clean it.

## LUBRICATION

■ Pay careful attention to the lubrication schedule for sanding tools. Because of the sanding dust, sanders often require more frequent lubrication than other power tools.

■ Avoid lubricating any *exposed* parts of a sander with oil. Oil attracts dust like a magnet, mixes with it, and forms a gummy substance that prevents the parts from operating properly. Unless oil is specified in the owner's manual, use graphite lubricants instead.

■ From time to time, wax *and* buff the platen of a belt sander to help the belt slide across it smoothly. Also wax and buff the work table, fence, and miter gauge. **Note:** It's extremely important to *buff* the wax after you apply it. Otherwise, the wax will mix with the sanding dust and form a gummy mess.

## CHANGING ABRASIVES

■ As abrasive belts and discs begin to load, clean them with a rubber abrasive cleaner. (*SEE FIGURE 4-15.*)

■ Don't overuse an abrasive; discard it as soon as it becomes dull, and mount a new one. If you continue to use worn belts, discs, or sandpaper, the grains will begin to drop off the backing material, often leaving deep scratches in the wood. The glue that once held the grains will begin to rub off on the wood and may interfere with the finish.

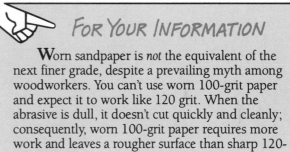

## FOR YOUR INFORMATION

**W**orn sandpaper is *not* the equivalent of the next finer grade, despite a prevailing myth among woodworkers. You can't use worn 100-grit paper and expect it to work like 120 grit. When the abrasive is dull, it doesn't cut quickly and cleanly; consequently, worn 100-grit paper requires more work and leaves a rougher surface than sharp 120-grit paper.

# SANDING SAFELY

**S**anding dust may be hazardous to your health. Several medical studies on cabinetmakers and furniture makers have linked *long-term* exposure to all types of sawdust with impaired breathing, chronic allergies, and respiratory diseases such as asthma and emphysema. Shorter exposure may aggravate these health problems if they already exist. Additionally, certain wood species are *toxic*, and their sanding dust may inflame the respiratory system or irritate the skin. (See "Toxic Woods and Potential Health Risks" on page 68 for a list of these species.)

Nor is this dust good for your tools. The wood fibers have mineral *extractives* imbedded in the cell walls. These act like a fine abrasive sand, wearing down the surfaces of moving metal parts with which they come in contact. And they contact more surfaces than you know — not even sealed ball bearings are immune, as any craftsman who has ever taken apart a worn bearing will testify. The dust eventually works its way around the seals.

For these reasons, you must control the sanding dust and avoid excessive exposure to it whenever you sand.

*(continued)* ▷

# SANDING SAFELY — CONTINUED

1   **Your best defense is to use** *dust collectors* with your sanding tools, vacuuming the dust as you work. This eliminates much of the sanding dust before it gets in the air or settles on your tools. Many tools come with collectors, while others offer them as optional accessories. For some sanding tools, you may have to make collectors. Here, a hollow box with a hole in the top and a vacuum outlet in the side collects dust from a sanding drum.

2   **You should also wear a dust** mask whenever you sand, even for short periods of time. A disposable paper mask is the least effective; a lot of fine dust sifts in around the sides. A close-fitting rubber mask with disposable or washable filters is much better, although many craftsmen find it uncomfortable in warm weather. And it may not work for craftsmen with beards and mustaches. The most effective and the most comfortable mask is a respirator helmet. This has a face shield that completely encloses the face while a small fan pumps in filtered air. They are expensive, but if you spend long periods sanding in a small room, they are worth the investment.

**3** **Forced *ventilation* greatly** reduces your exposure to sanding dust. A small window fan will move an enormous quantity of dusty air out of your shop in a short time.

**4** **You can make an effective *air scrubber*** from a box fan and a furnace filter. Set this on or near your workbench as you sand, or place it in the middle of your shop and keep it running all the time. Replace the filter or vacuum it whenever it looks dusty.

*(continued)* ▷

## SANDING SAFELY — CONTINUED

While prolonged exposure to *all* types of sawdust can be unhealthy, certain species may cause physical problems after a short exposure. These are classified as *toxic* woods.

Reactions to toxic woods fall into two categories — *respiratory* and *skin and eye* ailments. Respiratory problems include bronchial disorders, asthma, rhinitis, and mucosal irritations. Skin and eye reactions include dermatitis, conjunctivitis, itching, and rashes.

## TOXIC WOODS AND POTENTIAL HEALTH RISKS

| SPECIES | RESPIRATORY AILMENTS | SKIN AND EYE IRRITATION |
|---|---|---|
| Arborvitae | X | |
| Ayan | | X |
| Blackwood, African | | X |
| Boxwood | X | X |
| Cashew | | X |
| Cedar, Western Red | X | X |
| Cocobolo | | X |
| Cocus | | X |
| Dahoma | X | |
| Ebony | X | X |
| Greenheart | X | X |
| Guarea | X | |
| Iroko | X | X |
| Katon | X | |
| Lacewood | X | X |
| Lapacho | X | X |
| Mahogany, African | X | X |
| Mahogany, Honduras | X | X |
| Makore | X | X |
| Mansonia | X | X |
| Obeche | X | X |
| Opepe | X | X |
| Peroba Rosa | X | X |
| Peroba, White | X | X |
| Ramin | | X |
| Redwood | X | |
| Rosewood, Brazilian | | X |
| Rosewood, Indian | | X |
| Satinwood | | X |
| Sneezewood | X | |
| Stavewood | X | |
| Sucupira | | X |
| Teak | | X |
| Wenge | X | X |

# PRECISION SANDING JIGS

These shop-made sanding accessories help you achieve more precision and accuracy when you sand. A *notch jig* enables you to sand precise angles.

A *compass jig* lets you sand perfect circles. And a *pin-sanding jig* lets you reproduce sanded shapes exactly.

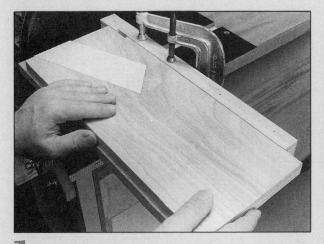

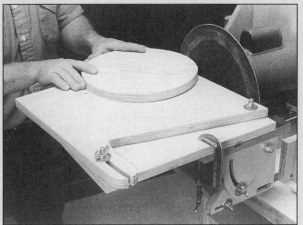

**1** **A *notch jig* holds a part at a** precise angle to the sanding disc or belt. Here, a notched board holds small frame parts to true the miter joints. A base, with a fence and stops, clamps to the work table. The fence guides the notch jig, and the stops halt it so the sanded frame parts will all be precisely the same size.

**2** **A *compass jig* provides a** pivot, allowing you to turn the stock as you sand it. The distance from the pivot to the abrasive is adjustable so you can sand a perfect circle to a precise diameter. Like the notch jig, this fixture has a base that clamps to the work table. A sliding arm lets you adjust the position of the pivot and lock it in place.

**3** **A *pin-sanding jig* lets you** sand the edges of any part to a precise size and shape on a drum sander. This, in turn, makes it possible to sand duplicate parts. The jig works much the same way as a pin router — make a pin the same diameter as the sanding drum, and position it directly beneath the drum. Also make a template the same size and shape as the parts you want to sand. Attach the template to the stock with double-faced carpet tape, then place the template on the base with the stock facing up. Sand the stock, tracing the shape of the template with the pin.

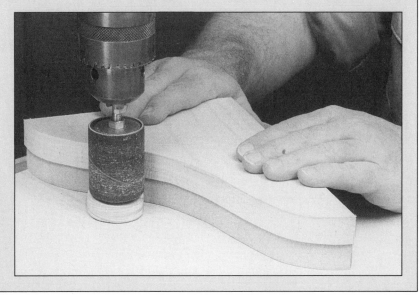

(continued) ▷

# PRECISION SANDING JIGS — CONTINUED

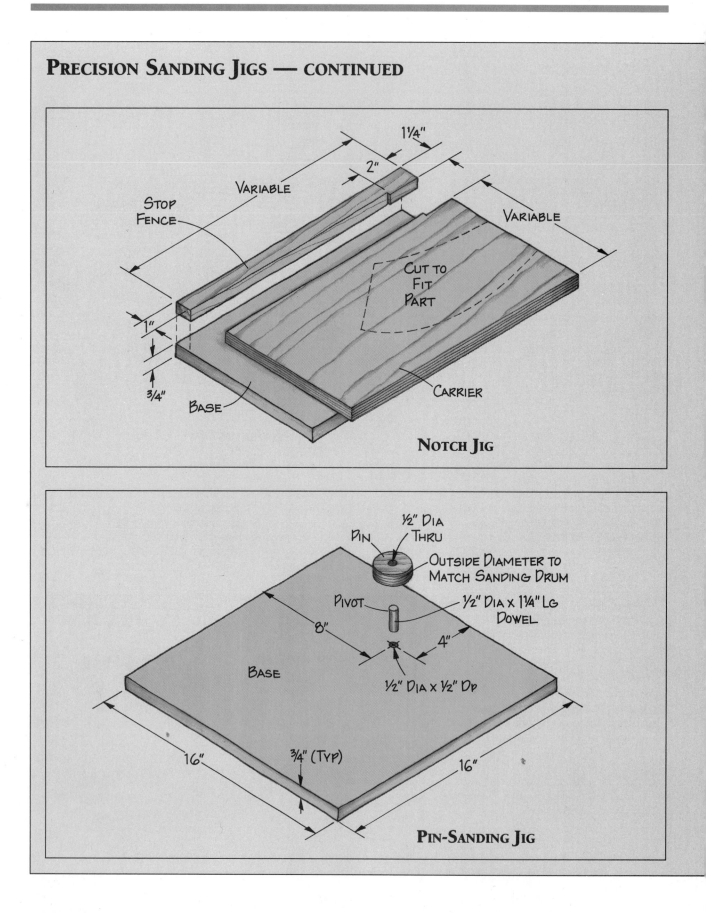

NOTCH JIG

PIN-SANDING JIG

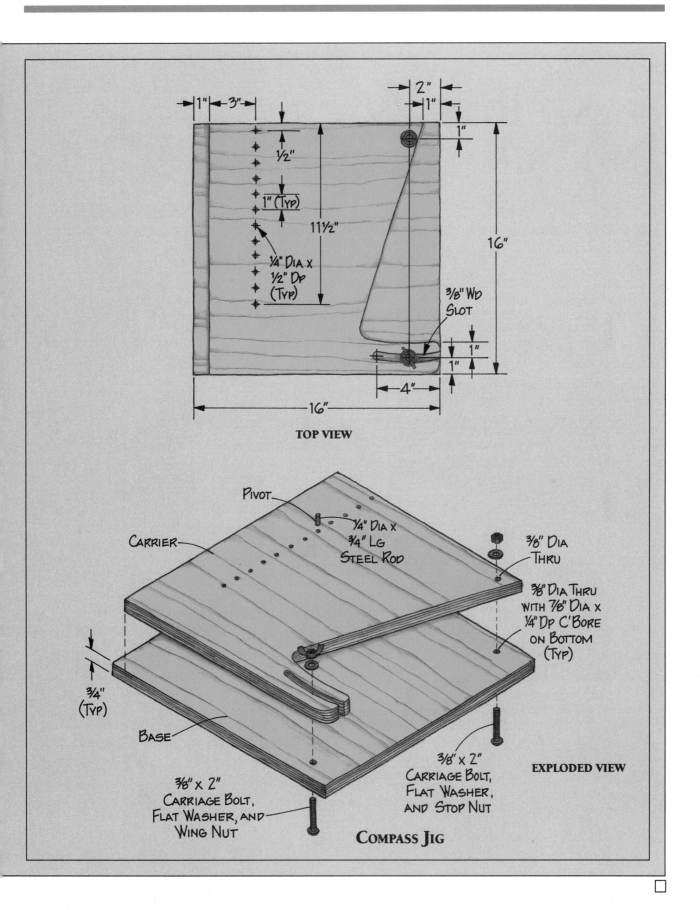

**TOP VIEW**

**COMPASS JIG**

**EXPLODED VIEW**

# 5

# Hand Planes, Files, and Scrapers

Jointers, planers, and sanders are by no means the only way to true and smooth a wood surface. Most craftsmen still rely on a few traditional hand tools — hand planes, files, and scrapers — for at least some surfacing chores.

Even if you use power tools for most of your planing and smoothing, there are still a few things that you just can't do without hand tools. And there are a few more that hand tools will do better.

# Hand Planes

## TYPES AND FEATURES

There are many types of hand planes, but only a fraction are concerned strictly with surfacing. These are the bench planes, block planes, palm planes, and spokeshaves. (*See Figure 5-1.*)

*Bench planes* have long, flat *soles*. The length of its sole determines a plane's purpose; shorter planes are used for smoothing rough stock, longer planes for flattening surfaces and jointing edges. Bench planes are two-handed tools. All-metal models have handles front and back; some wooden ones have a handle in front and a handrest on the back. The blade or *plane iron* is mounted with the bevel *down* on an adjustable *frog,* a mechanism that not only supports the blade but also allows you to adjust its position both front to back and side to side. The blade is covered with a cap iron or *chip breaker* to break up the shavings and keep

them from clogging the tool. The plane iron and chip breaker are held to the frog by a *lever cap.* (*See Figure 5-2.*) The parts that sandwich the plane iron reinforce it and make it extremely rigid. Because of this, a bench plane cuts smoother and with less effort than other types.

*Block planes* are smaller and shorter than bench planes. The plane iron is mounted with the bevel *up.* There is no frog or chip breaker; the iron is held directly to the body with a lever cap. Most block planes have an adjustable *mouth,* where the iron extends through the sole. By changing the size of this opening, you can control chatter and tear-out. The prevailing myth is that block planes are best for shaving end grain, but this isn't necessarily so. The cutting angles of a *standard* block plane and a bench plane are the

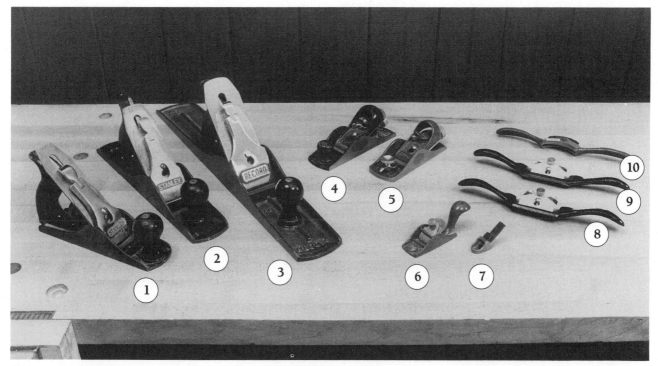

**5-1  Four common types of hand** planes are designed strictly for surfacing — bench planes, block planes, palm planes, and spokeshaves. Bench planes are distinguished by their length. A short bench plane, less than 11 inches long, is called a *smooth* or *scrub plane* (1) and is used mostly for surfacing rough stock. A *jack plane* (2), between 14 and 15 inches

long, is an all-purpose plane. A *jointer* or *try plane* (3) is over 18 inches long and is used for truing large surfaces and long edges. Block planes are characterized by the angle of the iron — a *standard block plane* (4) holds its plane iron at 20 degrees, while a *low-angle block plane* (5) holds it at 12 degrees. A *palm plane* (6) is defined by its size.

Some fit in the palm of your hand; others, known as *finger planes* (7), are so small they must be held between two fingers. Spokeshaves are made to plane narrow or round stock, and they differ in the shape of their sole. A *flat spokeshave* (8) has a flat sole; a *round spokeshave* (9) has a convex sole; and a *crescent spokeshave* (10) has a concave sole.

same, so neither has an advantage when cutting end grain. (*SEE FIGURE 5-3.*) Only a *low-angle* block plane has a slight advantage; its cutting angle is 8 degrees lower than either a bench plane or a standard block plane. The real benefit of a block plane is its size — it's designed to be used with one hand and is ideal for small surfacing jobs.

*Palm planes* are much smaller than block planes, and simpler in construction. (*SEE FIGURE 5-4.*) The plane iron, which is mounted with the bevel *down* as in a bench plane, is held directly to the plane body with a wedge or a screw cap. There is no apparatus for positioning the iron; you must tap the top end with a mallet to adjust the iron once it's mounted. If there is

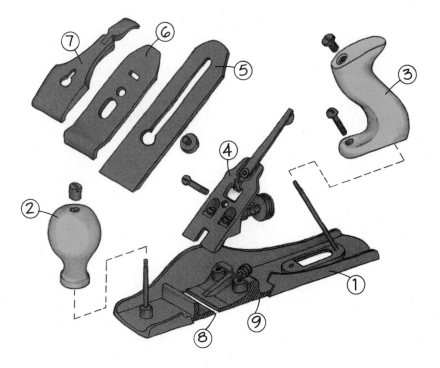

**5-2** The *body* (1) of an all-metal bench plane supports a *front handle* (2), a *rear handle* (3), and an adjustable *frog* (4). The frog holds the *plane iron* (5) and allows you to adjust its position. The iron is covered with a *chip breaker* (6), and a *lever cap* (7) holds the iron and the chip breaker to the frog. The cutting edge of the iron extends down through the *mouth* (8), a narrow opening in the bottom or *sole* (9) of the plane.

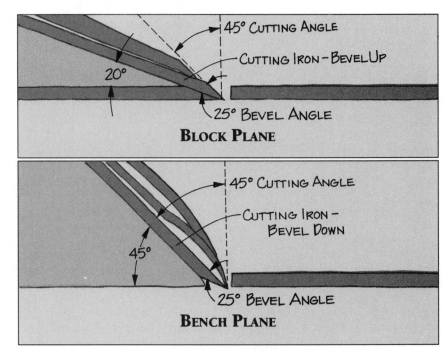

**5-3  A standard block plane holds** its plane iron at 20 degrees, while a bench plane holds it at 45 degrees. You might think that a block plane would slice the wood at a lower angle, but this isn't so. Because a block plane iron is mounted with the bevel up, and the iron in a bench plane is mounted bevel-down, the cutting angles are the same, as shown. Both bench planes and standard block planes are designed for general-purpose planing.

a handle, it's cast or carved as part of the body. Because of their small size, palm planes will reach places that bench planes and block planes won't. They are also useful for surfacing small areas.

*Spokeshaves* are designed to surface narrow and rounded stock such as table legs. The body has two long handles which protrude from each side. The plane iron is mounted between the handles and is held to the body with a screw cap. The sole is shaped to conform to the wood surface — it may be flat, convex, or concave. (SEE FIGURE 5-5.)

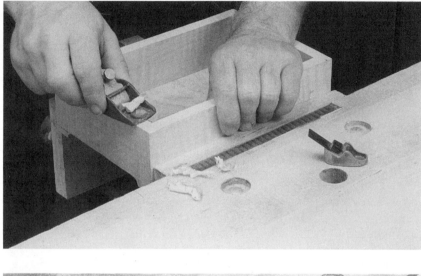

**5-4 Palm planes come in a** variety of sizes. The largest are a little smaller than a block plane and fit comfortably in the palm of your hand. The smallest must be grasped between two fingers and are, in fact, referred to as *finger planes*.

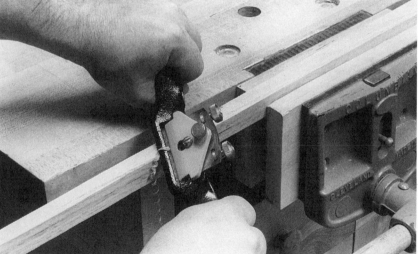

**5-5 Spokeshaves are specialized** planes, designed for smoothing and shaping narrow work. Unlike most other planing tools, which are pushed along the wood, spokeshaves are designed to be pulled or drawn toward you. Because of this, some woodworkers assume that they are similar to drawknives, but this is not so. Drawknives will split small pieces of wood or remove large amounts of stock, but cannot be used for surfacing. Spokeshaves remove just a little bit of stock at time, leaving a smooth surface.

## USING HAND PLANES

Before you use a hand plane to cut anything important, make sure the blade is sharp and properly adjusted. Few experiences in woodworking are more satisfying than cutting with a sharp plane, or more frustrating than trying to cut with a dull one. For most planes, the irons should be sharpened at 25 degrees; some craftsmen add a small microbevel to that. (SEE FIGURE 5-6.) If the plane has a chip breaker, set it 1/16 to 1/8 inch away from the cutting edge for rough work, or 1/32 to 1/16 inch away for fine work.

Secure the iron in the plane with the cutting edge parallel to the mouth opening but not protruding from the mouth. While passing the plane across a clear wood scrap, *slowly* advance the iron. For some planes, you simply turn a knob to advance the iron. For others, you must tap the top of the iron lightly with a mallet.

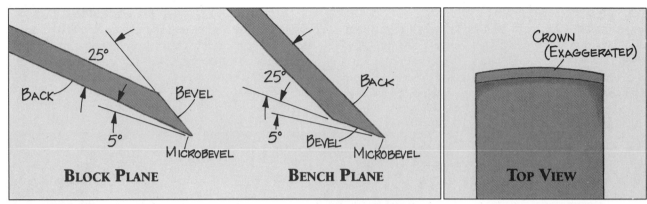

**BLOCK PLANE**   **BENCH PLANE**   **TOP VIEW**

**5-6  When properly sharpened,** the cutting edge of a plane iron should be *slightly* crowned. Many craftsmen also add a *microbevel* on the edge to help it stay sharp longer. Sharpen the iron at 25 degrees, using a sharpening guide to hold the angle precisely. Press down a little harder at the corners of the iron to create the crown. After the final honing, increase the angle to 30 degrees and make *two or three* light passes across the fine stone — no more — to make the microbevel. **Note:** When sharpening the iron of a block plane, make a 5-degree microbevel on the *back*. If you do it on the other side, you'll increase the cutting angle.

When the iron begins to take a shaving, check that it's cutting all across the width of the plane. (*SEE FIGURE 5-7.*) If not, readjust the angle of the iron. When the plane is cutting a paper-thin shaving as wide as the iron, it's ready to use.

When making *roughing cuts,* as you do when planing rough-cut lumber or removing a twist from a board, use a shorter plane and pass it across the wood at a steep diagonal to the wood grain. When making *smoothing cuts,* such as truing a surface or jointing an edge, use a longer plane. Hold it at a slight angle to the wood grain, but push the plane parallel to it. (*SEE FIGURE 5-8.*) *FIGURES 5-9 THROUGH 5-12* show some additional tricks for using a hand plane.

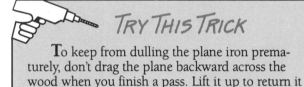

**TRY THIS TRICK**

**T**o keep from dulling the plane iron prematurely, don't drag the plane backward across the wood when you finish a pass. Lift it up to return it for the next pass.

To keep the plane gliding across the wood smoothly, wax and buff the sole with paste wax from time to time. Some craftsmen rub a candle or a block of paraffin wax lightly over the sole, then make a few passes on a wood scrap. This spreads out the wax and buffs it.

**5-7  It's just as important to** adjust the angle of the blade as its depth of cut. You know the depth of cut is correct when the plane is cutting a paper-thin shaving. You know the angle is correct when the plane is cutting a shaving as wide as the plane iron.

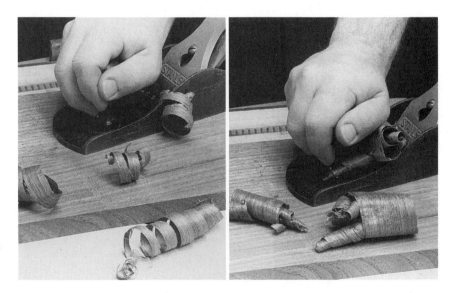

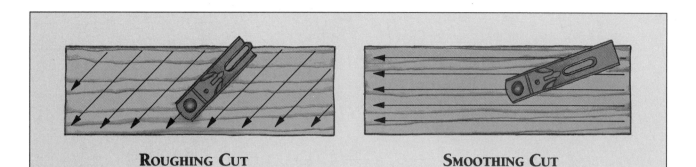

**ROUGHING CUT**

**SMOOTHING CUT**

**5-8 When you want to remove** stock from a board quickly, push the plane over the surface at a steep diagonal to the wood grain. This is called a *roughing cut,* and as the name implies, it does not leave a particularly smooth surface. When a smooth surface is important, make a *smoothing cut* — hold the plane at a slight diagonal to the wood grain and pass it across the surface parallel to the grain.

**BOARD TWISTED**

**BOARD CUPPED**

**BOARD FLAT**

**5-9 To remove a cup or twist from** a board, sight along a pair of *winding sticks* to help identify the high and low spots. Plane just the high spots until the winding sticks are parallel to one another and they sit flat on the wood.

**5-10 To plane a board to a** precise dimension, mark *all around* the outside of the board with a marking gauge, marking knife, or scratch awl. Then plane the wood down to the marks on all sides. If you're planing a face, check with a straightedge or a winding stick that the face is cut flat. If you are planing an edge, check with a square that it's cut square.

SCORE LINE
ALL AROUND
BOARD

**5-11 When planing a narrow** edge, keep the entire length of the plane on the edge, and the sole flat on the surface, even though you may hold the plane at a slight diagonal on the edge. Use your forward hand as a fence to help support the plane during the cut.

**5-12 Use a *shooting board* to help** plane the ends and edges of boards perfectly square. Lay the plane on its side so the cutting edge of the iron is vertical. Guide the sole along the fence, holding the wood against the plane and the stop at the back of the jig.

# FILES AND RASPS

Files cut the wood with row after row of wide teeth, like so many chisels stacked face to face. Rasps have hundreds of narrow teeth, like saw teeth, that bite into the wood. Generally, files are used for fine work, such as smoothing a surface, while rasps are used for rougher jobs where stock must be removed quickly.

## TYPES OF FILES

Files are classified in three ways — by how coarse or how fine they cut, by their tooth pattern, and by their shape.

*Cut* — The way in which a file cuts is determined by the spacing between the teeth. The more teeth per inch (tpi), the smoother the cut. The teeth on common files vary from 14 tpi (the coarsest) to 100 tpi

(the finest). Manufacturers rarely label their files according to the tpi, however. Instead, they divide them into three broad (and somewhat arbitrary) grades. From coarse to fine, these are *bastard cut, second cut,* and *smooth.* You can sometimes find additional grades among older files — *rough, coarse, dead smooth,* and *dead-dead-smooth.* Coarser grades cut quicker; finer grades cut smoother. Extremely fine files don't cut wood worth a darn because the teeth clog too quickly. These work better with metals.

*Tooth pattern* — The teeth are cut into the files in two different patterns, single-cut (parallel cutting edges) and double-cut (crossed cutting edges). (*SEE FIGURE 5-13.*) Of the two, the double-cut pattern usually works better in wood. Unless they're fairly coarse, single-cut files are better suited for metalworking.

**Note:** On most files, all the surfaces have teeth. But a few types have one or more *safe* edges, without any teeth.

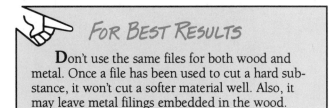

> ## FOR BEST RESULTS
>
> **D**on't use the same files for both wood and metal. Once a file has been used to cut a hard substance, it won't cut a softer material well. Also, it may leave metal filings embedded in the wood.

*Shapes* — Files are available in many shapes — flat, round, half-round, tapered, triangular — and these shapes often come in different sizes, with a variety of cuts and tooth patterns as well. Refer to "Files and Rasps" on page 83 for an illustrated list of the common shapes.

## TYPES OF RASPS

Rasps are classified in the same way as files — by cut, tooth pattern, and shape. Rasps, in fact, were once classified as a type of file with a *rasp-cut* tooth pattern.

*Cut* — There are just three grades of rasp cuts. The coarsest is a *wood rasp,* followed by a *cabinet rasp second cut,* and the finest, a *cabinet rasp smooth.*

*Tooth pattern* — Rasp teeth can be *machine stitched* or *hand stitched.* Machine stitching produces an even, geometric pattern, while hand stitching is completely random. (*See Figure 5-14.*) **Note:** The narrow edges of most rasps are made with file-like teeth or *angles.* Some have safe edges with no teeth.

*Shape* — Rasps are classified not only by the shape of their cross section, but also by the shape of the body. The bodies of many rasps are bent to fit curved surface or reach into small spaces. Refer to "Files and Rasps" on page 81 for an illustrated list.

## USE AND MAINTENANCE

Before using a file or rasp, mount the tang in a handle for better control and to keep the tang from puncturing your palm. Grasp the tool in two hands for good control — one hand on the handle, the other on the tip. (*See Figure 5-15.*) If you must grasp it with one hand, extend a finger or two along the upturned surface.

Remember that files and rasps are *cutting* tools; they do not scrape the wood surface like abrasives, as some novices assume. Consequently, they cut on the forward stroke *only.* You must lift the file out of the cut on the return stroke, as you do with a hand plane. If you maintain pressure on both the forward and the return strokes, you will dull the tool prematurely.

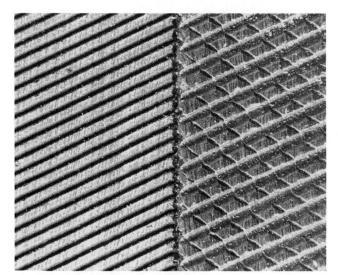

**5-13 On single-cut files, all the** teeth are parallel to one another. They appear as straight, uniform ridges. Double-cut files have two sets of parallel teeth, and each set is cut at an angle to the other so they form a crosshatch pattern.

**5-14 The teeth of a machine-** stitched rasp are arranged in an even pattern, while a hand-stitched rasp has no pattern — the teeth are randomly placed. Experienced woodworkers prefer hand-stitched rasps because they don't chatter as they cut and they leave a smoother surface. Unfortunately, they are also more expensive than the machine-stitched variety.

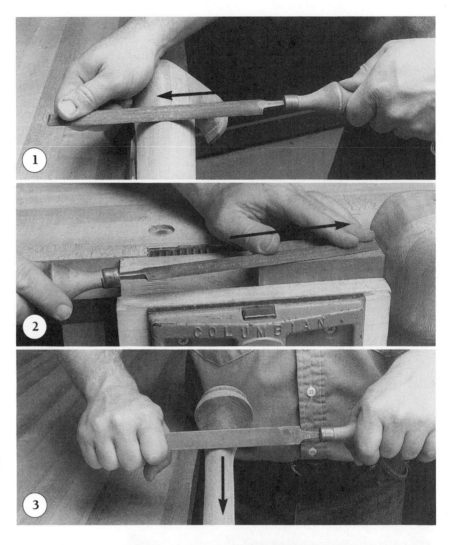

**5-15 There are three basic cuts** you can make with a file or rasp. When you *cross-file* (1) a workpiece, hold the tool perpendicular or at a diagonal to the wood grain and push it forward, across the grain. This will remove stock quickly. To *flat-file* (2), hold the tool parallel to the grain and push parallel to the grain. This makes a smoother cut. To *draw-file* (3), hold the tool perpendicular to the wood grain, but push it forward with the grain. This makes a finish cut.

Periodically, clean your files and rasps with a fine wire brush or *file card*. (SEE FIGURE 5-16.) When you're not using these tools, protect the cutting edges as you would the edges of fine chisels. Don't throw them in a drawer and let them bang into one another; this quickly ruins a fine file. Wrap them individually in scraps of cloth, make simple leather sheaths for them, or store them in the pockets of a canvas chisel wrap.

**5-16 When the teeth of a file or** rasp become clogged, clean them with a *file card*, brushing it over the tool parallel to the teeth. This card has hundreds of fine, stiff wire bristles that dig down between the teeth and remove the impacted wood fibers.

*TRY THIS TRICK*

**T**o prevent files and rasps from rusting, keep a camphor tablet with the wrapper partially opened in the drawer or cupboard with them. The camphor evaporates slowly and coats the metal with a thin, oily film that protects it from moisture.

# FILES AND RASPS

There are dozens of files and rasps, each with a different shape, cut, or tooth pattern. Some are designed for general work; others are made for one or two specific tasks. This chart lists those that are commonly used by woodworkers.

| COMMON WOODWORKING FILES | | |
|---|---|---|
| TYPE | DESCRIPTION | GENERAL USE |
| MILL | Single-cut, tapers along width and thickness; coarse mill files sometimes called *floats*. | Shaping, smoothing, and sharpening. |
| FLAT | Looks the same as a mill file, but has a double-cut. | Removing stock quickly. |
| HAND | Made the same as a flat file, but has a safe edge with no teeth. | Dressing corners where one adjacent surface must not be cut. |
| PILLAR | Double-cut, has two safe parallel edges. | Cutting slots. |
| HALF-ROUND | Double-cut, may have single-cut on round surface, tapers along width and thickness; coarse half-round files sometimes called *wood files*. | Cutting flat, convex, and concave surfaces. |
| CABINET | Same as half-round, but thinner with larger radius on round surface. | Cutting flat, convex, and concave surfaces. |
| THREE-SQUARE (TRIANGULAR) | Single-cut or double-cut, may be tapered or straight. | Single-cut for sharpening saw teeth, double-cut for dressing corners. |
| SQUARE | Double-cut, may be tapered or straight. | Cutting slots and dressing corners. |
| RAT-TAIL | Single-cut or double-cut, tapers at the end. | Dressing and enlarging holes, cutting concave surfaces. |

(continued) ▷

# FILES AND RASPS — CONTINUED

| COMMON WOODWORKING FILES | | |
|---|---|---|
| **TYPE** | **DESCRIPTION** | **GENERAL USE** |
| **AUGER BIT** | Single-cut, double-end with safe edges on one end. | Sharpening drilling tools. |
| **NEEDLE** | Can be single- or double-cut, very slender with long tangs, available in several shapes. | Dressing small or intricate work, sharpening. |

| COMMON RASPS | | |
|---|---|---|
| **TYPE** | **DESCRIPTION** | **GENERAL USE** |
| **WOOD** | Coarse teeth, tapers along width and thickness. | Quickly removing stock. |
| **CABINET** | Same as wood rasp, but has finer teeth and larger radius on round surface, often called *patternmaker's rasp*. | Shaping flat, convex, and concave surfaces. |
| **SCULPTING** | Same as cabinet rasp but with bent body. | Shaping and smoothing large carved or contoured surfaces. |
| **ROUND** | Tapers at the end. | Shaping concave surfaces, enlarging holes. |
| **RIFFLER** | Double-ended, curved body, available in several shapes. | Smoothing small carved or contoured surfaces, intricate work. |
| **CRANK-NECK** | Has offset tang. | Shaping and smoothing large surfaces. |
| **NEEDLE** | Very slender, tapered, available in several shapes. | Shaping and smoothing small or intricate work. |

# SCRAPERS AND SHAVEHOOKS

As the name implies, scrapers scrape the wood surface smooth. But unlike sandpaper, which uses abrasive grains with hundreds of microscopic cutting edges to scrape the wood, a scraper employs a thin metal blade with a long, sharp *burr* on its edge. This burr shaves the wood, then the blade plows up the cut fibers, removing a thinner-than-paper shaving from the wood surface. (*SEE FIGURE 5-17.*)

There are five types of scraping tools:

■ *Hand scrapers* are thin pieces of metal that come in various shapes, sizes, and thicknesses. (*SEE FIGURE 5-18.*)

■ A *cabinet scraper* mounts a blade in a rigid holder with handles on the sides. You cannot change the angle of the blade to the wood. (*SEE FIGURE 5-19.*)

■ A *scraper plane* mounts a blade in an adjustable holder, allowing you to change the blade angle. The holder is similar in size and shape to a small bench plane.

■ *Shavehooks* have metal blades attached to handles so you can pull them along the wood. The blades come in several different shapes. (*SEE FIGURE 5-20.*)

■ *Molding scrapers* are similar to shavehooks, but they are slightly smaller and the blades are more intricately shaped.

5-18 To use a **hand scraper,** hold the blade slightly off vertical, not quite square to the wood surface. Push or pull the blade forward, pressing down and varying the angle as you do so. When you feel the burr bite into the wood, hold that angle and continue to move the scraper forward as it cuts. Choose a blade to fit the surface you wish to scrape — straight for flat surfaces, curved for contoured surfaces. Many craftsmen prefer to hold hand scrapers in two hands, flexing the blade as they push it forward. However, this isn't a must. You can plane two-handed or one-handed, flexing or not flexing, whatever works best for the task at hand.

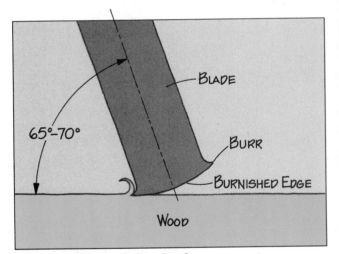

**5-17 Scrapers and shavehooks** each have a thin metal blade with a *burr* on the edge. The burr is turned 75 to 80 degrees from the face of the blade, so when the blade is held at a 65- to 70-degree angle to the wood, the burr shaves the surface. As the blade is pushed forward, it acts like a chipbreaker, turning the shaving and plowing it up. The rounded or *burnished* edge, just behind the burr, acts as a pressure bar and keeps the grain from tearing behind the cut. This lets you scrape a smooth surface on all sorts of wood grain and in any direction — it doesn't matter whether you scrape straight or figured grain.

**5-19 A cabinet scraper and a** *scraping plane* relieve some of the tedium of scraping. Holding and flexing a hand scraper can get tiresome when smoothing a large project. These tools hold the blade at the proper angle; all you have to do is push forward.

**5-20 Shavehooks and molding** *scrapers* are made to scrape in corners, shaped surfaces, and hard-to-reach areas. To use either tool, grasp the handle, push the blade down on the stock, and pull it toward you. Vary the angle of the blade by raising or lowering the handle. Shavehooks usually come in three shapes — triangle, square, and teardrop. Molding scrapers are available in a much wider variety.

The technique for using all of these tools is similar. Adjust or hold the blade at an angle to the surface, then push or pull it forward so the burr scrapes the wood. Don't drag the tool back across the surface of the wood on the return stroke; this will dull the burr. Lift it off the wood surface before returning it.

The real trick to using scrapers effectively is in *sharpening* them — you must raise a fine, even burr. The technique for raising a burr is slightly different for various scraping tools. For hand scrapers, you must remove the old burrs, file and grind the edge *square*, raise two separate burrs with a burnisher, and roll them over at the proper angle. (*SEE FIGURES 5-21 THROUGH 5-24.*) To sharpen the blades of cabinet scrapers, scraper planes, and shavehooks, you must remove the old burr, file and grind a slight *bevel* on the edge (between 60 and 45 degrees), raise a single burr, and roll it over.

(*SEE FIGURES 5-25 THROUGH 5-27.*) For molding scrapers, simply grind the face flat. (*SEE FIGURE 5-28.*)

When a scraper is properly sharpened, it will throw thin *curls,* similar to the shavings from a hand plane but much thinner. You know the scraper is dull when it won't produce anything but dust.

## A SAFETY REMINDER

Scrape as much as you can before you sand. Scraping takes less time than sanding and saves you the cost of the sandpaper. (A scraper leaves a finish comparable to 120- or 150-grit sandpaper.) More important, *scraping doesn't throw fine dust into the air.* You'll breathe in a lot less sawdust.

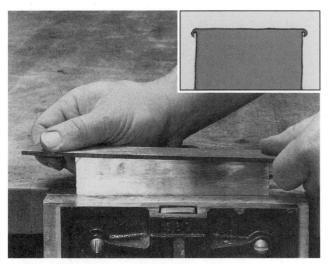

**5-21 To sharpen a hand scraper,** first file the cutting edges square to the face of the blade with a second-cut mill file. If the scraper is in good shape, this should only take a few strokes.

**5-22 After filing, hone the edges** with a medium sharpening stone, followed by a fine stone to remove any file marks. Wipe the faces on the fine sharpening stone to remove any traces of the old burr.

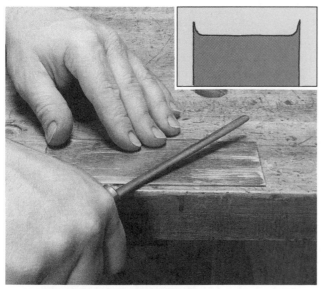

**5-23 Place the scraper flat on the** workbench. Lubricate the burnisher by rubbing it with a candle or a block of paraffin wax. Draw the waxed burnisher along each cutting edge, pressing down firmly enough that the burnisher makes a loud tick when it falls off the end of the scraper and hits the workbench. Turn the scraper over and repeat. This will raise two burrs on each edge, parallel to the face of the scraper. Some craftsmen call this *consolidating the edge*.

**5-24 Clamp the scraper in a vise** with the cutting edge up. Tilt the burnisher to the right or left, 10 to 15 degrees off horizontal, and draw it along the edge, pressing down firmly. Then tilt the burnisher in the other direction and draw it along the edge again. Turn the scraper over and repeat for the other cutting edge. This will roll the burrs over so they are between 75 and 80 degrees from the face. **Note:** The technique for sharpening the edges of curved hand scrapers is the same, although it takes more time and patience.

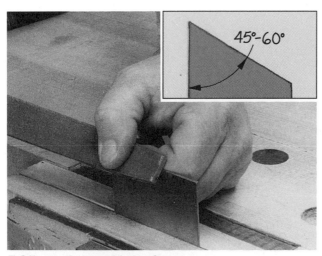

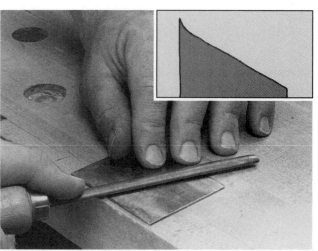

**5-25  To sharpen blades from** cabinet scrapers, scraper planes, and shavehooks, file and hone the cutting edge with a 60-degree bevel. **Note:** Some craftsmen prefer steeper bevels, up to 45 degrees, especially for cabinet scrapers and shavehooks.

**5-26  Place the blade flat on the** workbench. Lubricate the burnisher with wax and draw it along the cutting edge, pressing down firmly. This will begin to raise a small burr, parallel to the face of the blade.

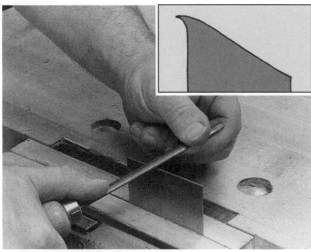

**5-27  Clamp the blade in a vise** with the bevel up. Holding the burnisher 30 degrees off horizontal, so it rests flat on the bevel, draw it across the cutting edge. Once again, press down firmly. Repeat several times, reducing the angle about 5 degrees with each pass, and stopping when the burnisher is at 15 degrees. This will roll the burr over to the proper angle. **Note:** If the blade doesn't cut as well as you think it should, experiment with different burr angles — roll the burr over a little more or a little less until it's cutting satisfactorily.

**5-28  To refresh the edge on a** worn molding scraper, simply grind the forward face flat on a sharpening stone. Keep grinding until all the arrises are sharp — none of the edges must be rounded over. A sharp metal edge will not cut as fast as an edge with a burr, but it still cuts a smooth surface.

# PROJECTS

# 6

# SCRAPER PLANE

A scraper plane combines the best features of a bench plane and a hand scraper. Like a scraper, it uses a blade with a burr to smooth the stock. You can scrape any wooden surface, no matter what the grain direction or pattern; the scraping blade will not dig in or chatter like an ordinary plane iron.

And like a bench plane, a scraper plane leaves the wood flat and true. The scraping blade does not follow the contours of the surface as a hand scraper does; the sole of the plane guides it to make a level cut.

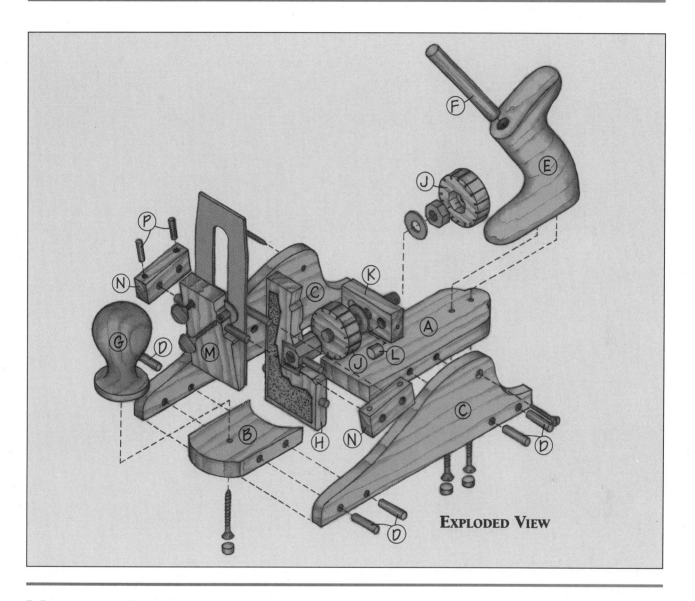

**EXPLODED VIEW**

# MATERIALS LIST (FINISHED DIMENSIONS)

## Parts

A. Back sole — ½″ x 2⅛″ x 6″
B. Front sole — ½″ x 2⅛″ x 3″
C. Sides (2) — ⅜″ x 2⅞″ x 9″
D. Side dowels (8) — ¼″ dia. x 1″
E. Back handle — 1″ x 3½″ x 5″
F. Handle reinforcing
   dowel — ⅜″ dia. x 5″
G. Front handle — 1⅝″ dia. x 2¾″
H. Blade
   support — ½″ x 2⅛″ x 4½″
J. Adjustor
   wheels (2) — 1½″ dia. x ½″
K. Adjustor bar — ½″ x 1″ x 2⅛″

L. Adjustor
   plugs (2) — ⅜″ dia. x ½″
M. Cap — ½″ x 2³⁄₁₆″ x 3¼″
N. Cap bars (2) — ⅜″ x ¾″ x 1⅞″
P. Cap bar reinforcing
   dowels (4) — ⅛″ dia. x ¾″

## Hardware

#10 x 1¾″ Flathead wood screws
   (3)
#8 x 1″ Flathead wood screws (2)
⅜″ dia. x 3″ Threaded rod
⅜″ Hex nuts (2)
#10 x 1″ Thumbscrews (2)
#10 T-nuts (2)
¼″ dia. x 2¹⁵⁄₁₆″ Steel rods (2)
¼″ dia. x 2⅝″ Steel rod
¼″ dia. x 2⅛″ Steel rod
2″ Plane iron
⁵⁄₁₆″ Washers (2)

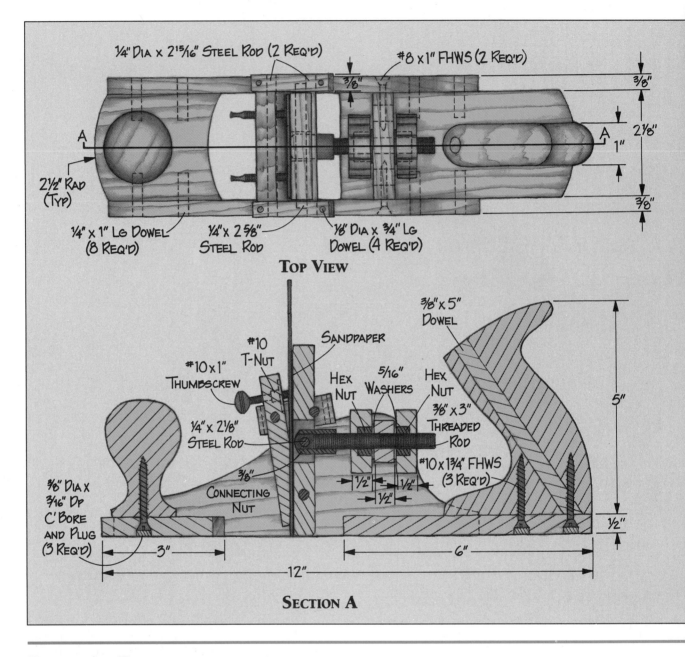

¼" DIA x 2¹⁵⁄₁₆" STEEL ROD (2 REQ'D)

#8 x 1" FHWS (2 REQ'D)

⅜"

⅜"

2⅛"

A

A

1"

2½" RAD (TYP)

⅜"

¼" x 1" LG DOWEL (8 REQ'D)

¼" x 2⅝" STEEL ROD

⅛" DIA x ¾" LG DOWEL (4 REQ'D)

**TOP VIEW**

#10 T-NUT

SANDPAPER

⅜" x 5" DOWEL

#10 x 1" THUMBSCREW

HEX NUT

5/16" WASHERS

HEX NUT

5"

¼" x 2⅛" STEEL ROD

⅜" x 3" THREADED ROD

⅜"

½"

½"

½"

#10 x 1¾" FHWS (3 REQ'D)

⅜" DIA x ³⁄₁₆" DP C'BORE AND PLUG (3 REQ'D)

CONNECTING NUT

3"

6"

12"

½"

**SECTION A**

# PLAN OF PROCEDURE

## 1 Select the stock and cut the parts to size.

This project requires less than 2 board feet of lumber — if you wish, you can make the plane from scraps. Whether you make it from new lumber or scraps, choose extremely hard wood, especially for the soles, blade supports, and cap. These parts must stand up to a lot of stress. On the plane shown, the soles, blade support, cap, adjustor bar, and adjustor wheels are made from cocobolo, a hard, dense tropical wood. The remaining parts are made from figured rock maple.

Select a scrap of 8/4 (eight-quarters) stock to make the handles. Cut a 2-inch-thick, 2-inch-wide, 4-inch-long turning block to make the front handle, and saw the back handle stock to the size specified in the Materials List.

Choose 4/4 (four-quarters) stock to make the remaining parts. Plane the stock to ½ inch thick, and cut the soles, blade support, cap, adjustor bar, and adjustor wheels to size. Plane the leftover stock to ⅜ inch thick, and make the sides and cap bars.

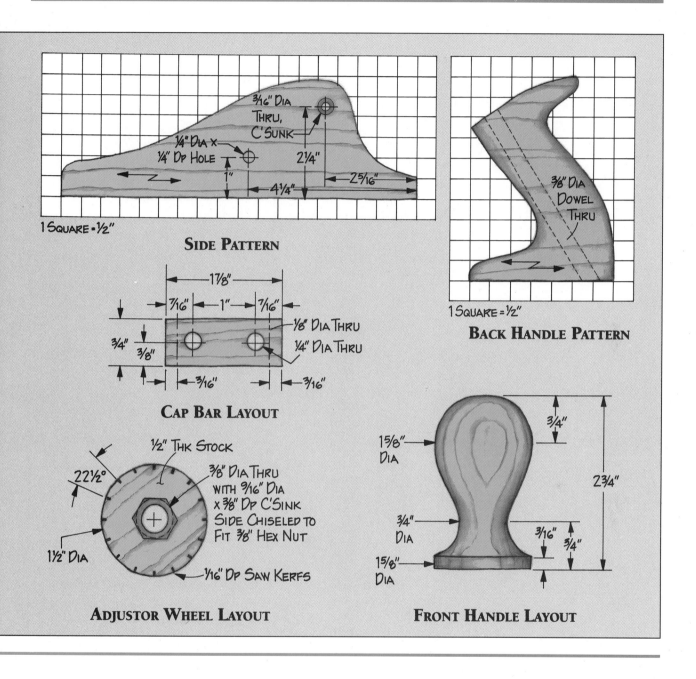

**SIDE PATTERN**

1 SQUARE = ½"

**CAP BAR LAYOUT**

**BACK HANDLE PATTERN**

1 SQUARE = ½"

**ADJUSTOR WHEEL LAYOUT**

**FRONT HANDLE LAYOUT**

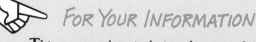

## FOR YOUR INFORMATION

This scraper plane is designed to use a 2-inch-wide plane iron from an ordinary jack plane. If you have a used-up blade, you can recycle it for this project. Most commercial scraper planes, however, mount 2¾-inch-wide cabinet scraper blades. If you would rather make a wider plane than shown here, increase the width of the soles, blade support,

and cap by ¾ inch. Cabinet scraper blades are available from:

Garrett Wade
161 Avenue of the Americas
New York, NY 10013
(800) 221-2942

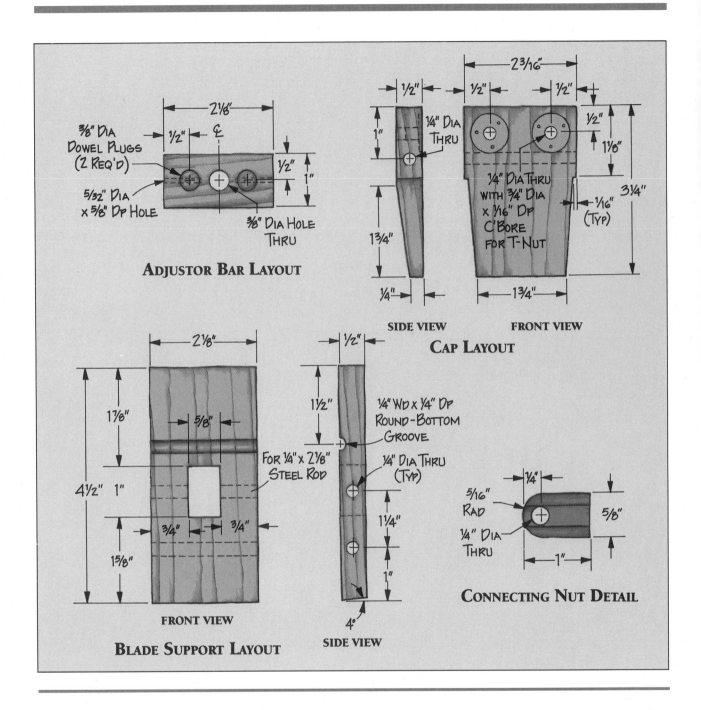

**ADJUSTOR BAR LAYOUT**

**CAP LAYOUT**

SIDE VIEW     FRONT VIEW

**BLADE SUPPORT LAYOUT**

FRONT VIEW     SIDE VIEW

**CONNECTING NUT DETAIL**

**2  Lay out the shapes of the parts.**  Fasten the side pieces face to face with double-faced carpet tape. Also tape the adjustor wheels and cap bars together. On the top board of the side stack, lay out the shape and the locations of the holes, as shown in the *Side Pattern.* Do the same for the adjustor wheels, following the *Adjustor Wheel Layout,* and the cap bars, following the *Cap Bar Layout.* Also lay out:

■ the back handle, as shown in the *Back Handle Pattern*

■ the blade support, as shown in the *Blade Support Layout*

■ the cap, as shown in the *Cap Layout*

■ the adjustor bar, as shown in the *Adjustor Bar Layout*

■ the soles, as shown in the *Top View*

**3  Drill the holes in the parts.**  Drill the holes, countersinks, and counterbores that you've marked on the parts. Drill the hole for the reinforcing dowel in the back handle with a spade bit or a long twist bit. *(SEE FIGURE 6-1.)* Also drill a ⁵⁄₈-inch-diameter hole in the blade support to remove most of the waste from the mortise.

**4  Cut the shapes of the parts.**  Using a band saw, scroll saw, or saber saw, cut the shapes of the sides, back handle, soles, adjustor wheels, and cap. Remember to cut a taper in the back face of the cap, as shown in the *Cap Layout/Side View.* With a scroll saw or rasp, enlarge the ⁵⁄₈-inch-diameter hole in the blade support to make the mortise. Cut ¹⁄₁₆-inch-deep saw kerfs around the circumference of the adjustor wheels, as shown in the *Adjustor Wheel Layout,* to help you get a better grip when you use them. Sand the sawed edges of all the stacked parts, then take them apart and discard the tape.

**5  Rout the groove in the blade support.**  The cap assembly pivots in a ¹⁄₄-inch-wide round-bottom groove in the back of the blade support. Rout this groove with a table-mounted router and a veining bit.

**6  Sculpt and turn the handles.**  Glue the reinforcing dowel in the back handle stock. When the glue dries, sculpt the handle with a rasp and file. *(SEE FIGURE 6-2.)* Turn the front handle on a lathe, or, if you don't have a lathe, sculpt it with a rasp and file, too.

**7  Round over the end of the connecting nut.** Mark the position of the ¹⁄₄-inch-diameter hole in the connecting nut, and drill it with a twist bit. Cut the nut to the proper length with a hacksaw, then grind the radius on the end with a disc sander or strip sander. *(SEE FIGURE 6-3.)* To check the radius, temporarily mount the nut in the blade support with a ¹⁄₄-inch-diameter steel rod. Hold the scraper blade against the front of the support and pivot the nut up and down. If the nut rubs the blade at any point, grind the radius a little more.

*Try This Trick*

Finish sand the contoured handles with flutter sheets or a flap sander.

**6-1  To drill the ³⁄₈-inch-diameter** hole in the back handle stock for the reinforcing dowel, clamp the stock in a hand screw at an angle, aligning the layout lines for the hole with the bit. Using a long twist bit or spade bit, bore the hole as deep as you can — on most drill presses, this will be 4 inches or less. Turn off the drill press and, with the bit still in the hole, raise the work table about 2 inches. Turn on the drill and complete the hole.

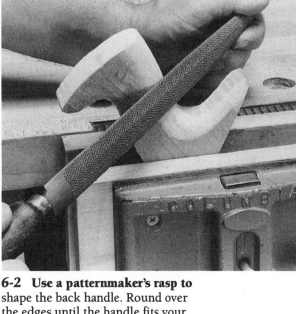

**6-2  Use a patternmaker's rasp to** shape the back handle. Round over the edges until the handle fits your hand, then smooth the surface with a cabinet file. If you wish, you can shape the front handle in the same way.

**8** **Assemble the plane.** Temporarily assemble the parts of the plane to check their fit and operation. Stick the sides and the handles to the soles with double-faced carpet tape. When you're satisfied all the pieces go together and work properly, take the plane apart and finish sand the wooden surfaces. Be careful not to round over any edges that will be joined to other parts.

Assemble the blade support, the connector nut, and the two shortest steel rods. Glue the sides to the soles with the blade support mounted in the stopped holes. Reinforce the glue joints with ¼-inch-diameter, 1-inch-long dowels, as shown in the *Top View*. When the glue dries, joint the soles and the bottom edges of the sides flat. Then glue the front and back handles to the soles, reinforcing the joints with flathead wood screws. Countersink and counterbore the screws, then cover the heads with plugs made from the same wood as the soles.

Using a chisel, cut the sides of the counterbores in the adjustor wheels to fit ⅜-inch hex nuts. Glue the nuts in the wheels with epoxy cement. Also glue ⅜-inch-diameter plugs in the adjustor bar, as shown in the *Adjustor Bar Layout*. **Note:** These plugs provide a solid purchase for the screws that hold the bar to the sides. Screws don't hold well in end grain, and without the plugs, the screws might work loose or split the bar.

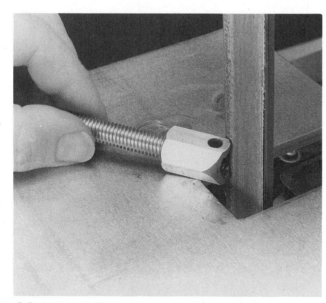

**6-3 To grind the radius on the** end of the connecting nut, mount the nut on the end of the threaded rod. Use the rod to hold and guide the nut while you grind away the stock.

Turn the threaded rod into the connector nut, tightening it against the steel rod that runs through the nut. Turn an adjustor wheel onto the rod with the nut facing away from the blade support. Place a flat washer over the rod, then the adjustor bar, then another washer. Finally, turn the second adjustor wheel onto the rod with the nut facing toward the blade support. Drive flathead wood screws through the sides and into the adjustor bar. Tighten the screws so they're snug, but not so tight that the adjustor bar won't pivot.

Glue the T-nuts in the cap with epoxy cement. Also glue the reinforcing dowels in the cap bars (with ordinary white or yellow glue). Assemble the cap, cap bars, and long steel rods, gluing the ends of the rods in the cap bars with epoxy. *Don't* glue the cap bars to the cap; the bars should pivot. Turn the thumbscrews into the nuts in the cap, and mount the blade and cap assembly on the blade support.

**9** **Finish the scraper plane.** Remove the blade, cap assembly, and adjustor assembly. Take the adjustor assembly apart and remove the thumbscrews from the cap. Set the hardware aside, do any necessary touch-up sanding, and apply several coats of tung oil to the wooden surfaces. After the finish dries, rub it out with wax and buff it.

Glue or stick 120-grit abrasive to the front face of the blade support — this will help prevent the blade from slipping. Sharpen the blade, then reassemble the plane.

**TIPS FOR USING THE SCRAPER PLANE**

■ Sharpen and maintain the blade as you would any cabinet scraper — grind the bevel to between 45 and 60 degrees and turn a single burr on the edge. Mount the blade with the burr facing forward and the bevel facing back.

■ To position the blade, turn the adjusting screws until the blade support leans forward 5 to 10 degrees off vertical. Set the plane on a flat surface, loosen the cap, and position the blade so the edge rests flat on the surface. Tighten the cap screws to lock the cap in place. Slowly tilt the blade support forward as you make test passes on a wood scrap. The blade will begin to bite into the wood more and more. When the plane is plowing up wide, thin curls, the blade is properly positioned.

■ The farther you tilt the blade forward, the deeper it will bite — up to a point. Once you tilt it past 20 degrees (approximately), it begins to recede again. Use a shallow tilt to remove stock quickly, and a steep tilt for ultrasmooth cuts.

# 7

# THICKNESS SANDER

A thickness sander performs the same task as a thickness planer — it makes one surface of a board parallel to another. But instead of cutting, it *sands* the wood. Sanding to thickness takes longer than planing, but it's gentler on the wood. The abrasive does not lift the grain like planer knives, and consequently there is no chip-

ping or tear-out. This allows you to surface thin and highly figured wood, as well as rough, resawed, and glued-up stock.

A shop-made thickness sander is also gentler on your wallet than a planer. You can build this machine from ordinary materials for about one-tenth the cost of most 12- and 15-inch thickness planers. Yet it

provides a larger capacity and the same accuracy. As designed, the sander will surface boards 3 to 4 inches thick and 16 inches wide. You can adjust the depth of cut with precision down to $1/128$ inch, and the sanded board will be uniform in thickness to within just a few thousandths of an inch.

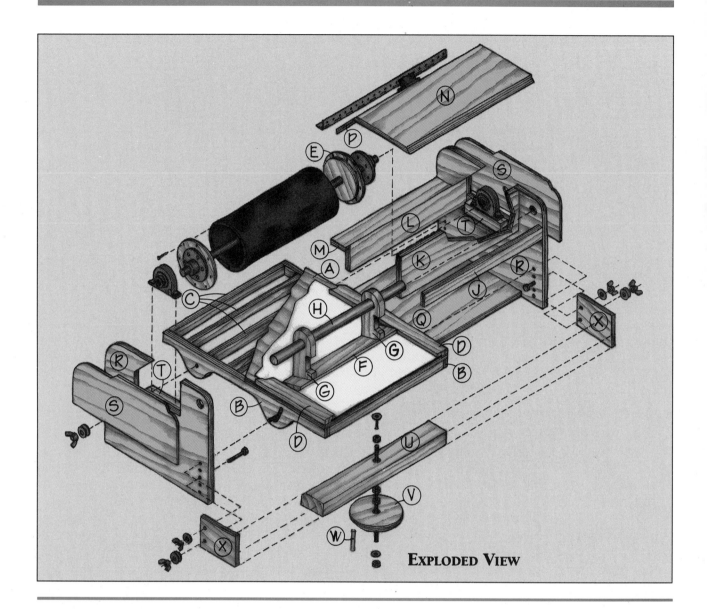

**EXPLODED VIEW**

# MATERIALS LIST (FINISHED DIMENSIONS)

## Parts

A. Work table*   ¾″ x 20¼″ x 28″

B. Table struts (2) ¾″ x 3⅝″ x 28″

C. Table
   ribs (11)   ¾″ x 1¼″ x 18¾″

D. Guides† (2)   ¾″ x 1¾″ x 28″

E. Drum ends (2)   6⅝″ dia. x ¾″

F. Anti-kickback
   foot†   ¾″ x 3⅛″ x 16″

G. Anti-kickback
   arms (2)   ¾″ x 3″ x 7⅛″

H. Anti-kickback
   rod†   1¼″ dia. x 21¹¹⁄₁₆″

J. Anti-kickback
   rail   ¾″ x 1¹¹⁄₁₆″ x 20¼″

K. Infeed rail   ¾″ x 6″ x 20¼″

L. Vertical outfeed
   rail   ¾″ x 3¾″ x 20¼″

M. Horizontal outfeed
   rail   ¾″ x 4¼″ x 20¼″

N. Top cover   ¾″ x 10″ x 21¾″

P. Dust cover   ¾″ x 4⅝″ x 20³⁄₁₆″

Q. Bottom   ¾″ x 15″ x 20¼″

R. Sides (2)   ¾″ x 15¼″ x 18″

S. Side covers (2) ¼″ x 7¾″ x 18″

T. Pillow block
   mounts† (2)   1½″ x 1½″ x 6″

U. Elevator
   rail†   1½″ x 3¾″ x 21¾″

V. Elevator wheel   6″ dia. x ¾″

W. Elevator
   handle†   ½″ dia. x 3″

X. Elevator
   mounts (2)   ¾″ x 4⅜″ x 5⅞″

*Make this part from medium-density
fiberboard (MDF), Baltic birch plywood,
or Apple-ply plywood.
†Make these parts from solid hardwood.

## MATERIALS LIST — CONTINUED
### Hardware

³/₈″ x 2″ Lag screws (4)

#12 x 1″ Flathead wood screws (12)

#6 x 1¼″ Flathead wood screws (16)

#10 x ¾″ Panhead wood screws (4)

#8 x 1″ Ovalhead wood screws (16)

#6 x 2″ Utility screws (110)

½″ x 2½″ Hex bolts (4)

½″ x 2½″ Carriage bolts (2)

½″ x 8⁷/₈″ Threaded rod

½″ Hex nuts (4)

½″ Wing nuts (6)

½″ x 1¼″ Fender washers (10)

⁷/₁₆″ Flat washer

⁵/₁₆″ Flat washers (4)

#8 Finishing washers (16)

1½″ x 16″ Piano hinge and mounting screws

⁵/₈″ dia. x 36″ Steel shaft

6″ I.D. x 16″ Schedule 80 PVC pipe (Purchase 18″–20″ length, then cut to size.)

⁵/₈″ I.D. Locking ball bearing pillow blocks (2)

⁵/₈″ I.D., 3¾″ O.D. Lathe face-plates‡ (2)

2¼″ I.D. Flange ferrule‡ (dust chute)

18¾″ x 28″ Heavy-duty plastic laminate

‡*This hardware is available from:*
*Total Shop*
*P.O. Box 25429*
*Greenville, SC 29616*

## PLAN OF PROCEDURE

**1   Select the stock and cut the parts to size.**
To make this project, you need approximately one-half sheet of cabinet-grade ³/₄-inch plywood, a scrap of ¼-inch plywood, 2 board feet of 4/4 (four-quarters) hardwood, 2 board feet of 8/4 (eight-quarters) hardwood, a 1¼-inch-diameter, 36-inch-long hardwood dowel, and a quarter sheet of medium-density fiberboard (MDF), Baltic birch plywood, or Apple-ply plywood. On the thickness sander shown, most of the structural parts are made from birch-veneer plywood or maple hardwood. The work table is made from Baltic birch plywood and covered with laminate.

Cut the parts to the sizes shown in the Materials List. Bevel the edges of the top cover, dust cover, and vertical outfeed rail, and chamfer the elevator rail, as shown in *Section A*. Cover the top surface of the work table with plastic laminate, leaving bare a ³/₄-inch-wide strip along each edge. Secure the laminate with contact cement, then *immediately* finish the bottom surface edges and the bare strips of the top surface with tung oil. This will prevent the table from warping.

**2   Lay out the shapes of the parts and the locations of the slots and holes.**   Several of the parts in this project are duplicates of one another. You can save time by sticking these parts together face to face with double-faced carpet tape, and machining both parts at the same time. Stack these parts:

- Table struts
- Drum ends
- Anti-kickback arms
- Sides
- Side covers
- Elevator mounts

Lay out the shapes of any parts that aren't simple rectangles, marking the top part of each stack, and include the locations of all holes and slots:

- the table struts, as shown in the *Table Strut Layout*
- the drum ends, as shown in the *Sanding Drum Assembly/End View*
- the anti-kickback arms, as shown in the *Anti-kickback Arm Layout*
- the dust cover, as shown in the *Dust Cover Layout*
- the sides, as shown in the *Side Layout*
- the side covers, as shown in the *Side Cover Layout*
- the elevator rail, as shown in the *Elevator Detail* and *End View*
- the elevator wheel, as shown in the *Elevator Wheel Layout*
- the elevator mounts, as shown in the *Elevator Detail*

### FOR YOUR INFORMATION

**T**he sander is designed so it can be mounted to an ordinary stand with a motor *or* to a multipurpose tool such as a Shopsmith or a Total Shop. If you plan to mount this machine to a multipurpose tool, lay out the sides with the cutout shown in the *Multipurpose Tool Mount Detail*.

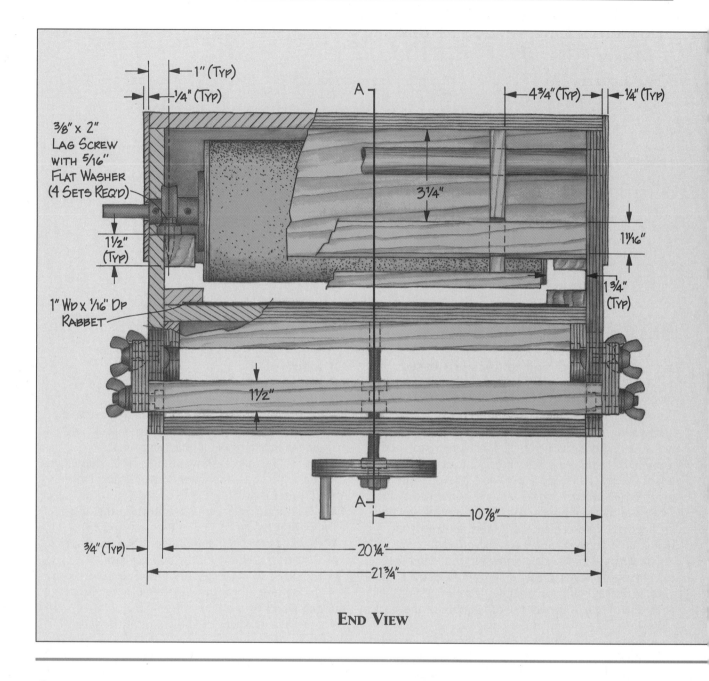

**END VIEW**

**3** **Drill the holes in the parts.** Drill the holes, countersinks, and counterbores that you've marked on the table struts, drum ends, anti-kickback arms, dust cover, sides, side covers, elevator bar, elevator wheel, and elevator mounts. Also drill holes to mark the ends of the slots in the table struts.

**4** **Cut the shapes of the parts.** Using a band saw, scroll saw, or saber saw, cut the shapes of the table struts, drum ends, anti-kickback arms, sides, side covers, and elevator wheel. Sand the sawed edges,

then take apart all the stacked parts that you have cut and drilled, and discard the tape.

**5** **Cut the slots in the table struts.** Using a straight bit and a hand-held router, rout ½-inch-wide slots in the table struts. Note that these slots are *curved*. For this reason, use a *Circle-Routing Jig* to guide the router. *(SEE FIGURE 7-1.)* You can also make these slots by cutting out the waste between the holes that mark the ends of the slots using a coping saw, saber saw, or scroll saw.

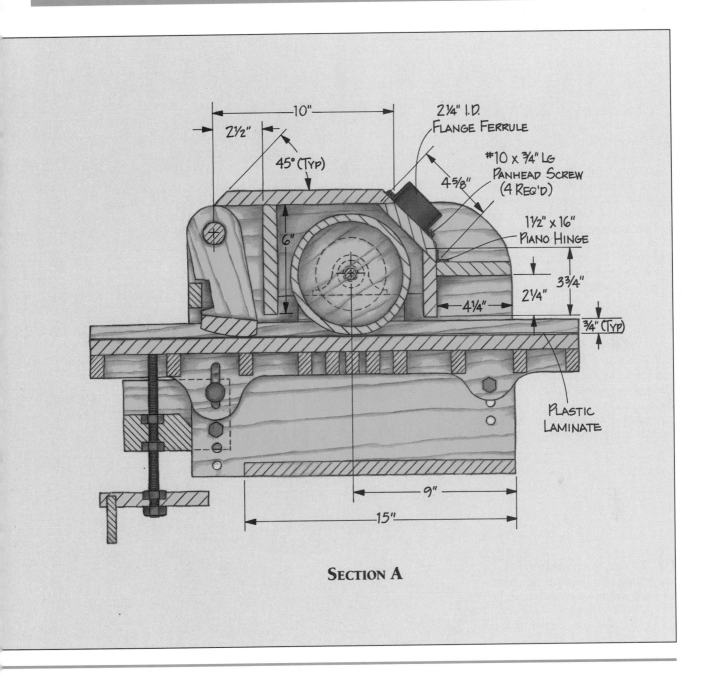

**SECTION A**

**6  Cut the rabbets in the guides and drum ends.**
Using a router or a dado cutter, cut 1-inch-wide, 1/16-inch-deep rabbets in the edges of the guides for the laminate, as shown in the *End View*.

Countersink the holes in the lathe faceplates, then fasten them to the drum ends with #12 flathead wood screws, centering the 5/8-inch-diameter holes in the faceplates over the 3/4-inch-diameter holes in the ends. Using a table-mounted router, cut 5/16-inch-wide, 1/2-inch-deep rabbets around the circumference of the drum ends. (*SEE FIGURE 7-2.*)

**7  Shape the anti-kickback foot.**  Mark the shape of the anti-kickback foot on both ends of the stock, as shown in the *Anti-Kickback Foot Profile*. Using a bench plane, round over the bottom face of the foot, shaving away the stock until you reach the profile marks. (*SEE FIGURE 7-3.*)

**8  Assemble the thickness sander housing.**
Lightly sand the pieces of the housing — sides, rails, bottom, pillow block mounts, and anti-kickback parts. Glue the pillow block mounts to the inside surfaces

**7-1   Use this simple circle-routing**
jig to rout the curved slots in the
table struts. Mount the router to the
jig, then insert a $1/2$-inch-diameter
bolt through the hole in the small
end of the jig and the pivot hole in
one strut. Place the strut on a scrap
of plywood and clamp both the strut
and the scrap to the workbench.
(The scrap will keep you from routing your workbench.) Place the
router bit in either hole that marks
an end of the slot. Adjust the depth
of cut so the bit will cut just $1/16$ to $1/8$
inch into the strut. Hold the router
securely, turn it on, and swing
toward the hole that marks the other
end of the slot. Stop cutting when
you reach that hole. Stop the router,
readjust the depth of cut — lowering
the bit another $1/16$ to $1/8$ inch — and
rout again. Repeat until you have cut
the slot completely through the strut.

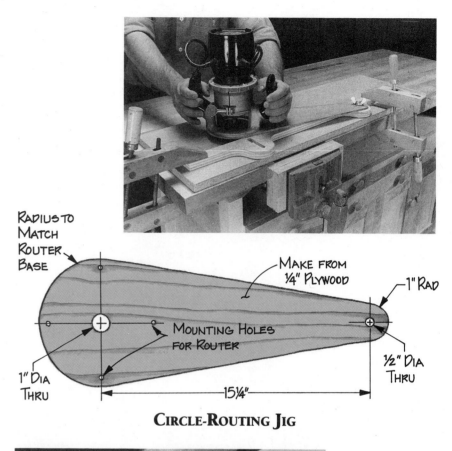

**CIRCLE-ROUTING JIG**

**7-2   To rout the rabbets in the**
drum ends, use a pivot jig to guide
the work. Mount a $1/2$-inch straight
bit in a table-mounted router, and
clamp the jig to your router table so
the distance between the center of
the pivot and the cutting edge of the
bit is precisely 3 inches. Adjust the
depth of cut so the router will cut
about $1/16$ inch into the stock. Turn
the router on, and place a drum end
over the pivot with the lathe faceplate
up. Slowly lower the drum end until
the router bit bites into the wood,
then turn the drum end on the pivot.
When you have cut all around the
circumference, turn off the router,
remove the drum end, and readjust
the depth of cut to go another $1/16$
inch deeper. Repeat until you have
cut the rabbet to the desired depth.

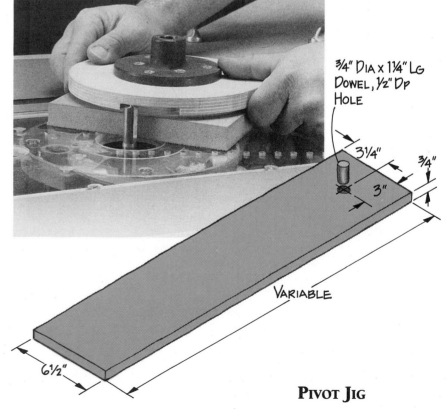

**PIVOT JIG**

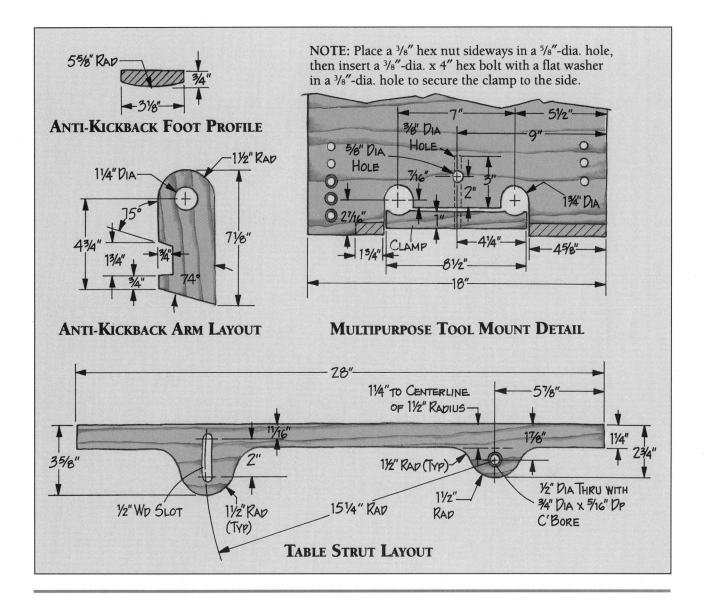

**ANTI-KICKBACK FOOT PROFILE**

5⅝" RAD    ¾"    3⅛"

**ANTI-KICKBACK ARM LAYOUT**

1¼" DIA    1½" RAD    15°    4¾"    1¾"    ¾"    ¾"    7⅛"    74°

**MULTIPURPOSE TOOL MOUNT DETAIL**

NOTE: Place a ⅜" hex nut sideways in a ⅝"-dia. hole, then insert a ⅜"-dia. x 4" hex bolt with a flat washer in a ⅜"-dia. hole to secure the clamp to the side.

7"    5½"    ⅜" DIA HOLE    9"    ⅝" DIA HOLE    7⁄16"    3"    2"    1¾" DIA    2⁷⁄16"    1"    CLAMP    4¼"    4⅝"    1¾"    8½"    18"

**TABLE STRUT LAYOUT**

28"    1¼" TO CENTERLINE OF 1½" RADIUS    5⅞"    ¹¹⁄16"    1⅞"    1¼"    3⅝"    2"    1½" RAD (TYP)    2¾"    ½" WD SLOT    1½" RAD (TYP)    15¼" RAD    1½" RAD    ½" DIA THRU WITH ¾" DIA x ⁵⁄16" DP C'BORE

of the sides, as shown in the *Side Layout*. Let the glue dry, then assemble the sides, anti-kickback rail, infeed rail, vertical outfeed rail, horizontal infeed rail, and bottom with glue and utility screws. Also fasten the anti-kickback foot to the anti-kickback arms with glue and screws. Countersink all screws, but countersink and counterbore the screws that you use to attach the foot to the arms. Plug the screw holes, and sand the plugs flush.

Insert the anti-kickback rod through a 1¼-inch-diameter hole in one of the sides. Hold the anti-kickback assembly in place, and push the rod sideways through the arms and the hole in the opposite side. Check that the anti-kickback assembly swings freely, and screw the arms to the rod.

**7-3 Use a bench plane to round** over the bottom face of the foot. Mark the radius on both ends, then shave the stock down to the marks.

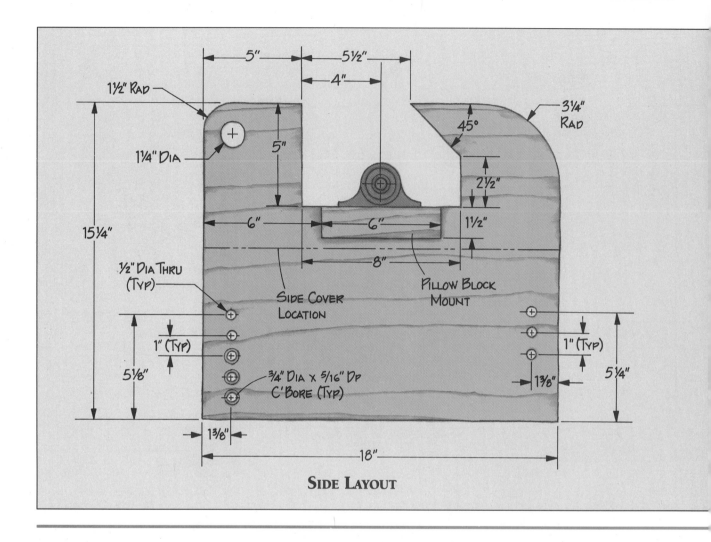

**SIDE LAYOUT**

**9  Assemble the table.** Lightly sand the parts of the table assembly — struts, ribs, guides, and the bottom surface of the table. Assemble the parts with utility screws. Drive the screws that hold the ribs to the table from the bottom.

Using a hacksaw, cut the 2½-inch-long hex bolts to 1¾ inches long. Put the table between the sides and insert two bolts through the pivot holes in the struts, then through the sides near the outfeed end of the housing. Secure the bolts with wing nuts and fender washers. Turn the nuts tight enough to draw the heads of the bolts into the counterbores.

Insert carriage bolts through the slots in the struts, then through the sides near the infeed end of the housing. Secure the bolts with wing nuts and fender washers, but don't tighten the nuts. Test the tilting action of the table. It should travel up and down smoothly. If it binds, enlarge the slots with a file.

## FOR YOUR INFORMATION

**Y**ou may be wondering why you have to cut the bolts. Why not just buy bolts of the proper length? Because 1¾-inch-long bolts are threaded all along their length. The threads will rub inside the holes, enlarging them. The fit will become sloppy, and the sander will lose some of its accuracy. The longer bolts are only partially threaded. After you cut them to length, the unthreaded portion of the shafts will rest in the holes.

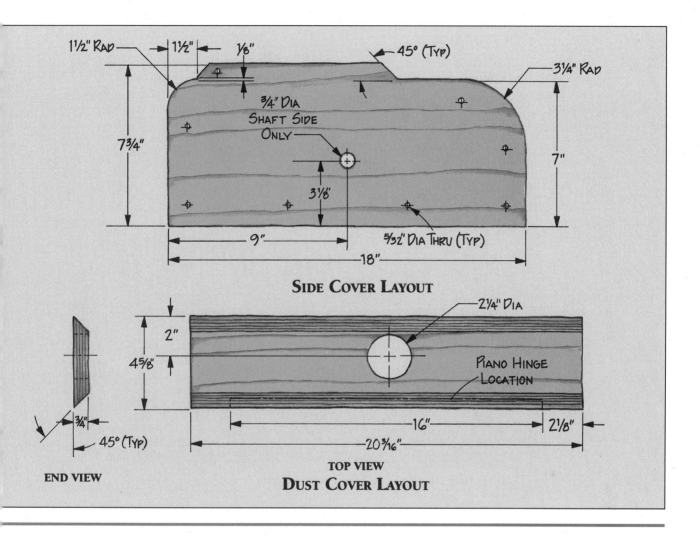

**SIDE COVER LAYOUT**

**END VIEW**

**TOP VIEW**
**DUST COVER LAYOUT**

## 10   Assemble and mount the sanding drum.

Cut the PVC pipe to length. As you do, make sure that the ends of the pipe are square to the sides. If not, file or sand them square. Glue the drum ends to the sides with epoxy cement. Reinforce these joints by drilling and countersinking holes around the circumferences of the drum ends and driving #6 flathead screws through the ends and into the plastic drum.

Cut the steel shaft to the length needed. This will depend on how you intend to power the sander, and on the pulley or the coupling you will use. Insert the steel shaft through the faceplates on the assembled drum. Place the pillow block over the ends, then tighten down the setscrews in the faceplates and the blocks.

Loosen the setscrews and remove the shaft. The screws will have left tiny indentations in the shaft surface. Using a grinder or a file, cut flats at these marks, as shown in the *Shaft Layout*. Replace the shaft in the

drum, replace the pillow blocks over the ends, and tighten the setscrews on the flats.

Place the assembled drum in the housing so the pillow blocks rest on their mounting blocks. Secure them to the mounting blocks with lag screws.

## 11   Assemble the table elevator.

Lightly sand the parts of the elevator — rail, wheel, handle, and mounts. Attach the mounts to the rail with glue and screws, and glue the handle in the wheel.

Press a ½-inch hex nut into each of the counterbores in the elevator rail. (*SEE FIGURE 7-4.*) Also press a nut into the counterbore in the elevator wheel. Fasten the wheel to the end of the threaded rod with a flat washer and another hex nut, as shown in the *Elevator Detail*. Thread a wing nut onto the rod, place a fender washer over the nut, and thread the rod through the rail.

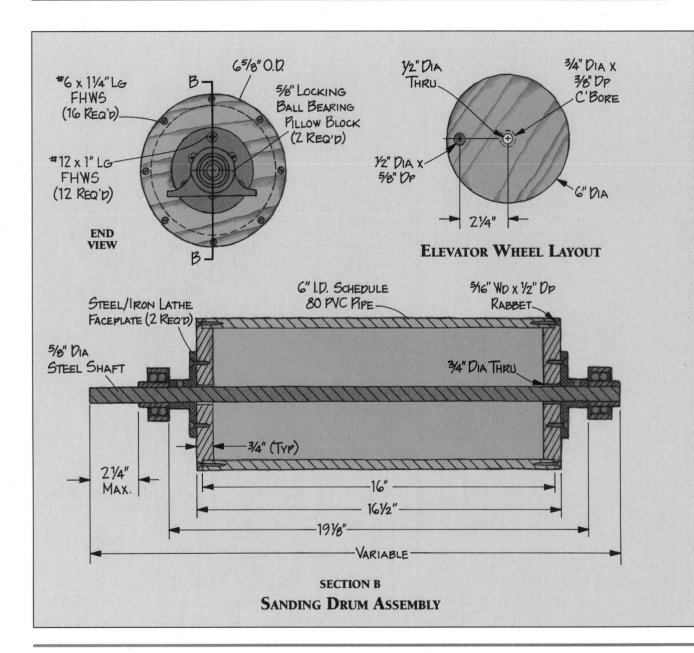

#6 x 1¼" LG
FHWS
(16 REQ'D)

#12 x 1" LG
FHWS
(12 REQ'D)

B

6⅝" O.D.

5⅛" LOCKING
BALL BEARING
PILLOW BLOCK
(2 REQ'D)

**END
VIEW**

B

½" DIA
THRU

¾" DIA X
⅜" DP
C'BORE

½" DIA X
⅝" DP

6" DIA

2¼"

**ELEVATOR WHEEL LAYOUT**

STEEL/IRON LATHE
FACEPLATE (2 REQ'D)

6" I.D. SCHEDULE
80 PVC PIPE

⁵⁄₁₆" WD X ½" DP
RABBET

⅝" DIA
STEEL SHAFT

¾" DIA THRU

¾" (TYP)

2¼"
MAX.

16"

16½"

19⅛"

VARIABLE

**SECTION B
SANDING DRUM ASSEMBLY**

**7-4  Thread two ½-inch hex nuts**
onto the rod and turn them so they
are exactly 1½ inches apart. (The
outside edge of each nut should be
flush with the faces of the elevator
rail.) Mark the sides of the nuts that
face you. Set these nuts in the rail so
the marked sides face in the same
direction, then thread the rod through
the bar. Don't worry if the fit seems
tight; this is as it should be.

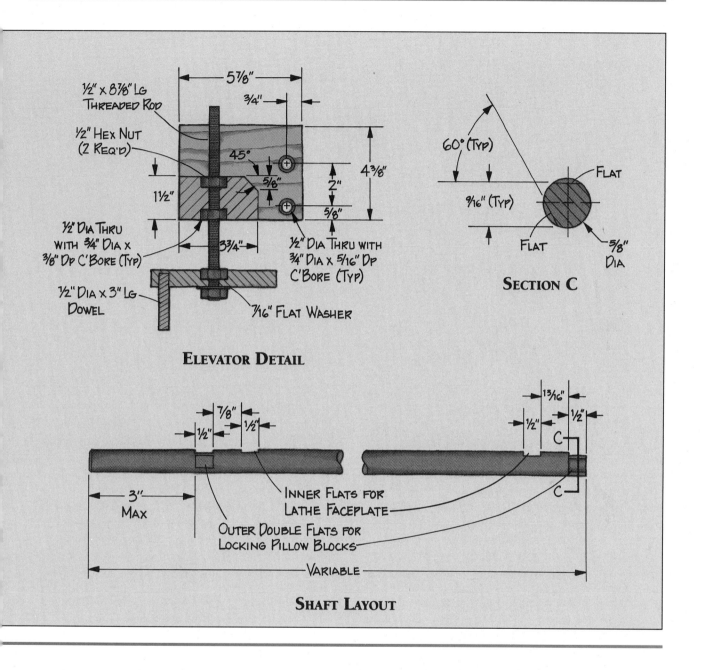

**½" x 8⅞" LG THREADED ROD**

**½" HEX NUT (2 REQ'D)**

5⅞"

¾"

45°

5/8"

1½"

4⅜"

2"

5/8"

**½" DIA THRU WITH ¾" DIA x ⅜" DP C'BORE (TYP)**

3¾"

**½" DIA THRU WITH ¾" DIA x 5/16" DP C'BORE (TYP)**

**½" DIA x 3" LG DOWEL**

**7/16" FLAT WASHER**

**ELEVATOR DETAIL**

60° (TYP)

9/16" (TYP)

FLAT

FLAT

5/8" DIA

**SECTION C**

13/16"

7/8"

½"

½"

½"

½"

C

C

3" MAX

**INNER FLATS FOR LATHE FACEPLATE**

**OUTER DOUBLE FLATS FOR LOCKING PILLOW BLOCKS**

VARIABLE

**SHAFT LAYOUT**

Remove the carriage bolts, washers, and nuts that hold the table to the infeed side of the housing. Put the elevator assembly in position, and insert the carriage bolts through the table struts, the sides, and the *top* holes in the elevator mounts. Insert hex bolts through the sides and the *bottom* holes in the mounts. Secure all the bolts with fender washers and wing nuts, then tighten the nuts on the hex bolts to draw the heads into the counterbores.

**12 Assemble and attach the covers.** Lightly sand the covers. Attach the top cover to the dust cover with glue and utility screws. Place the top assembly on the housing and fasten it to the horizontal outfeed rail with a piano hinge. (The top assembly must open easily, allowing you to reach inside the housing.) Fasten a flange ferrule to the dust cover with panhead screws, centering the ferrule over the 2¼-inch-diameter hole in the cover.

Fasten the side covers to the sides with ovalhead screws and finishing washers. Note that the top screws in the side covers lock the top assembly in place. To open the top, you must remove these screws. Remember to replace the screws before you use the sander.

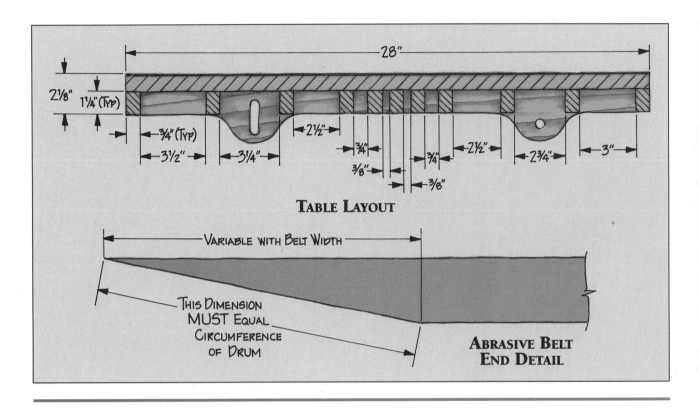

**TABLE LAYOUT**

VARIABLE WITH BELT WIDTH

THIS DIMENSION
MUST EQUAL
CIRCUMFERENCE
OF DRUM

**ABRASIVE BELT
END DETAIL**

**13 Mount the sander and connect it to a motor.** If you have elected to mount this sander on a multipurpose tool, clamp it to the way tubes and connect it to the power takeoff on the headstock. Adjust the speed changer to run at about 1,100 rpm.

To mount the sander to a stand, drive lag screws through the bottom and into the stand's top. Use a 1,725-rpm induction motor, rated for *at least* 1 horsepower, to drive the sander. (Less powerful motors will bog down.) Connect the tool to the motor with pulleys and a V-belt, using a 4-inch-diameter pulley on the sanding drum shaft and a 2½-inch-diameter pulley on the motor. This will run the sander at approximately 1,100 rpm.

**14 True the sanding drum.** The sanding drum must be perfectly round and concentric on its shaft. If it isn't, the sander will shake and vibrate as it runs and the wood won't be sanded evenly. To true the drum, cut a scrap of ¾-inch plywood 16½ inches wide — it should just fit between the guides. Using spray adhesive, stick a strip of 40- or 50-grit sandpaper across the width of the plywood.

Place the plywood in the sander so the abrasive is directly under the sanding drum. Clamp the plywood to the work table, turn on the sander, and *slowly* raise the table until it contacts the drum.

Don't sand the drum aggressively. If you raise the table too fast, the PVC pipe will heat up and expand; after you think you've sanded the drum true, it will cool down and shrink out of round. Instead, raise the table for just a few seconds, letting the abrasive sand the drum, then lower the table for a few seconds more to give the drum time to cool. Continue in this fashion, raising and lowering the table until you have sanded the entire surface of the drum and it's running true.

**15 Finish the thickness sander.** Take the sander off its stand. Remove the covers and detach the sanding drum, table assembly, and elevator assembly from the housing. Remove all the hardware from the wooden parts and set it aside. Do any necessary touch-up sanding on the wooden surfaces, then apply several coats of tung oil. After the finish dries, wax and buff the work table and any surfaces that rub together. This will help the sander operate smoothly.

**16 Reassemble the thickness sander.** Replace the table assembly, elevator assembly, and sanding drum in the housing. Attach the covers, then mount the completed sander on its stand or multipurpose tool, and connect it to the motor.

**17** **Cover the sanding drum and the anti-kick-back foot with abrasive.** Purchase a 4-inch-wide roll of *cloth-backed* abrasive. (Paper-backed abrasive is difficult to remove from the drum when it wears out.) Open the top cover so you can easily reach the sanding drum. Trim the leading end of the abrasive belt as shown in the *Abrasive Belt End Detail*. Note that the angled edge of the belt is equal to the circumference of the drum. If you want to use a wider or narrower belt, the angle will change but the length of the angled edge won't — always cut the edge equal to the circumference.

Tape the leading end to the drum, then wind the abrasive onto the drum. When the drum is completely covered, mark the trailing end of the belt. Unwind the belt from the drum and trim the trailing end — it should be a mirror image of the leading end. Spray the drum and the back of the abrasive belt with a rubber-based adhesive such as contact cement. Let the adhesive dry to develop sufficient tack, then wind the abrasive onto the drum. (SEE FIGURE 7-5.)

Also cover the bottom surface of the anti-kickback foot with abrasive, again using a rubber-based adhesive to secure the sandpaper.

**7-5 Cover the drum by winding** an abrasive belt onto it. To get the belt started properly, trim its leading end so the angled edge is equal to the circumference of the drum. Be careful not to overlap the edges of the belt as you wind it — it's better to have gaps between the edges than to have them overlap.

## TIPS FOR USING THE THICKNESS SANDER

■ Use only coarse sandpaper for thicknessing, no finer than 50 grit — fine sandpaper may clog. For smoothing, you can use finer grades, up to 100 grit.

■ The elevator will move the table vertically just over 1 inch at the sanding drum. However, by mounting the table and elevator assemblies in different holes in the housing, you can move the table up to 4 inches (3 inches if the sander is mounted on a multipurpose tool). When setting up for thicknessing stock, run the elevator down to its lowest position, then mount the table and elevator so the surface of the stock is within 1 inch of the sanding drum when you slide it through the tool. Use the elevator to make further adjustments.

■ To raise or lower the table with the elevator, loosen the wing nuts on the carriage bolts, turn the elevator wheel, then tighten the wing nuts again. *The nuts must be tight before you use the sander!*

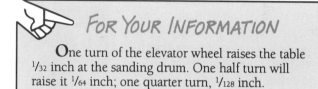

## FOR YOUR INFORMATION

**O**ne turn of the elevator wheel raises the table $1/32$ inch at the sanding drum. One half turn will raise it $1/64$ inch; one quarter turn, $1/128$ inch.

■ Don't try to remove too much stock at once; the machine will bog down and the paper will clog. Also, the drum may heat up, expand, and distort. Remove a maximum of $1/32$ inch at a time from softwood and narrow hardwood boards, $1/64$ inch from wide hardwood boards.

■ When surfacing rough or uneven stock, carefully adjust the tool to remove the *high spots* first. If you come to a high spot you hadn't anticipated, turn off the sander and lower the table before continuing. Remember, remove no more than $1/32$ inch at a time.

■ Hook up a shop vacuum to the sander while you work. Otherwise, the sawdust will build up inside the machine.

■ Periodically raise the top cover and clean the drum with a rubber abrasive cleaning stick. Remember to secure the cover before using the machine.

## A SAFETY REMINDER

**K**eep all the covers in place when using the machine, and never reach inside the housing when the sanding drum is running. When changing the abrasive or maintaining the tool, unplug it or disconnect it from its motor.

# 8

# DISC-AND-DRUM SANDER

A disc sander smooths flat and convex surfaces; a drum sander smooths concave surfaces. Combined, they make a wonderfully useful machine for both rough and precision sanding tasks. Use a disc-and-drum sander to remove saw marks, true miter joints, fit parts, smooth curves, adjust the shapes of contours, and carry out dozens of other sanding operations.

You can build this benchtop disc-and-drum sander with a double-shaft motor — an electric motor with a shaft that protrudes from both ends. Secure the disc to one end of the shaft, and the drum to the other, and fashion work tables for both the disc and the drum. This shop-made machine is just as capable as many commercial stationary tools, yet it remains light enough to move easily. Store it under your workbench or in a cabinet when it's not in use; clamp it to the bench or a stand when it is.

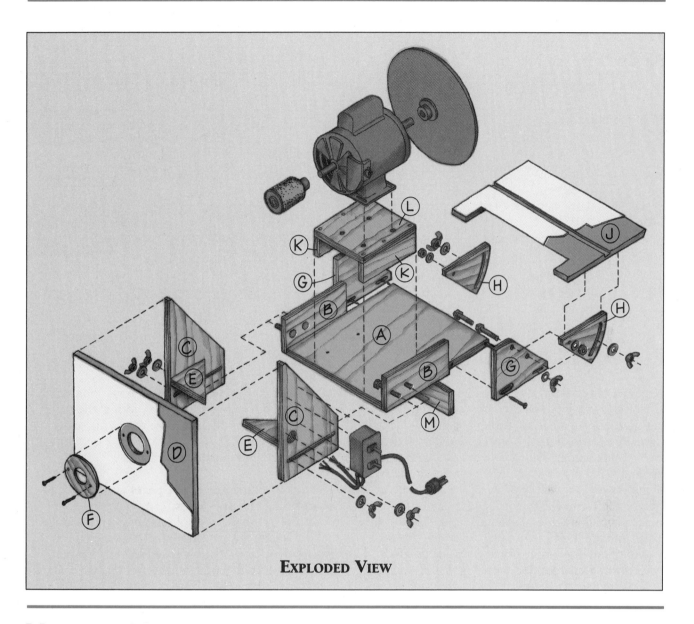

**EXPLODED VIEW**

# MATERIALS LIST (FINISHED DIMENSIONS)

## Parts

A. Base           ³/₄" x 13" x 14¹³/₁₆"

B. Drum table
   mounts (2)      ³/₄" x 4" x 7¹/₂"

C. Drum table
   sides (2)       ³/₄" x 7¹/₂" x 13¹/₂"

D. Drum table*    ³/₄" x 13¹/₂" x 16"

E. Drum table
   braces (2)      ³/₄" x 4⁷/₈" x 4⁷/₈"

F. Drum table
   inserts (5)     3¹/₂" dia. x ¹/₄"

G. Disc table
   mounts (2)      ³/₄" x 5³/₄" x 7¹/₈"

H. Disc table
   trunnions (2)   ³/₄" x 4¹¹/₁₆" x 6"

J. Disc table*    ³/₄" x 10³/₄" x 16"

K. Motor
   mounts (2)      ³/₄" x 2" x 7¹/₄"

L. Motor base     ³/₄" x 8" x 7¹/₄"

M. Clamp bar
   (optional)      ³/₄" x 2¹/₄" x 10"

*Make these parts from plywood, medium-density fiberboard (MDF), or a laminate-covered sink cutout.

## Hardware

¹/₄" x 1¹/₂" Lag screws (6)

#14 x 2" Flathead wood screws (2)

#10 x ³/₄" Flathead wood screws (2)

#10 x ¹/₂" Panhead screws (2)

#6 x 1³/₄" Utility screws (30)

³/₈" x 2¹/₄" Hex bolts (8)

⁵/₁₆" x 1¹/₂" Carriage bolts (4)

¹/₄" x 2" Hanger bolts (2)

³/₈" Wing nuts (6)

¹/₄" Wing nuts (2)

(continued) ▷

## MATERIALS LIST — CONTINUED

### Hardware – CONTINUED

⁵⁄₁₆″ Hex nuts (4)
¼″ Hex nuts (2)
³⁄₈″ Stop nuts (2)
³⁄₈″ x 1¼″ Fender washers (6)
¼″ x 1″ Fender washers (8)
⁵⁄₁₆″ I.D. Flat washers (6)
¼″ I.D. Flat washers (2)
Heavy-duty plastic laminate (4 sq. ft. — optional)
Single-outlet steel electrical box
Solid outlet box cover
Box grounding screws (2)
Straight 1″ cord clamps (2)

Right-angle 1″ cord clamp
#14-3 SJT Electrical cord (10′)
#14-2 SJT Electrical cord (2′)
Grounded plug
Double-pole, single-throw (on/off) switch
Double-pole, double-throw (reversing) switch
#14–16 Center splices (4)
#14–16 Ring terminals (17)
½-hp, 1,725-rpm Reversible double-shaft motor*
12″ Sanding disc†

2¼″ x 3″ Sanding drum†
½″ Drill chuck† (optional)

*These motors are available from many electrical supply stores. Look in the Yellow Pages under "Electric Motors." Look for one with a standard (NEMA 56) frame.
†These accessories are made to mount on a ⁵⁄₈-inch-diameter arbor. They are available from:

> Total Shop
> P.O. Box 25429
> Greenville, SC 29616

## PLAN OF PROCEDURE

**1** **Select the materials and cut the parts to size.** To make this project, you need approximately one half sheet (10 square feet) of cabinet-grade ³⁄₄-inch plywood, a scrap of ¼-inch plywood, and a laminate-covered sink cutout. This sink cutout will make the disc and drum tables. If you wish, substitute Baltic birch plywood, Apple-ply plywood, or medium-density fiberboard (MDF) for the sink cutout. All these materials are more stable than a particleboard cutout and are less likely to warp, but you'll need a small piece of heavy-duty plastic laminate to cover their working surfaces. The tables on the disc-and-drum sander shown are made from laminate-covered Baltic birch plywood.

Cut the parts to the sizes shown in the Materials List. Also cut the chamfer in the end of the disc table, as shown in the *Disc Table Layout*. If you are making the tables from plywood or MDF, cover the top surfaces with plastic laminate. Secure the laminate with contact cement, then immediately finish the uncovered surfaces of the tables with tung oil. (It's also a good idea to finish the bottom surfaces if you make the tables from a sink cutout.) This will prevent the bottom surface from absorbing more moisture than the top. When this happens, the bottom surface expands more than the top, and the table warps.

**Note:** Before cutting the motor mounts to size, rest the motor on the workbench and measure the distance between the bench top and the center of the arbor. For a motor with a standard frame, this distance will be 3½ inches. If you've purchased a nonstandard motor, you will have to adjust the width of the motor mounts to compensate. When the motor sits on its assembled mount, the distance from the base to the center of the arbor must be 6¼ inches.

**2** **Lay out the shape of the parts and the locations of the slots and holes.** Several of the parts in this project are either duplicates or mirror images of one another. You can save time by sticking these parts together face to face with double-faced carpet tape and machining both parts at the same time. Stack these parts:

- Drum table mounts
- Drum table sides
- Drum table braces
- Drum table inserts
- Disc table mounts
- Disc table trunnions

Lay out the shapes of any parts that aren't simple rectangles, as well as the locations of all holes and slots. For those parts that you've stacked, just mark the top part in each stack and lay out:

- the drum table, as shown on the *Drum Table Layout*
- the drum table mounts, as shown in the *Drum Table Mount Layout*
- the drum table sides, as shown on the *Drum Table Side Layout*
- the disc table, as shown on the *Disc Table Layout*

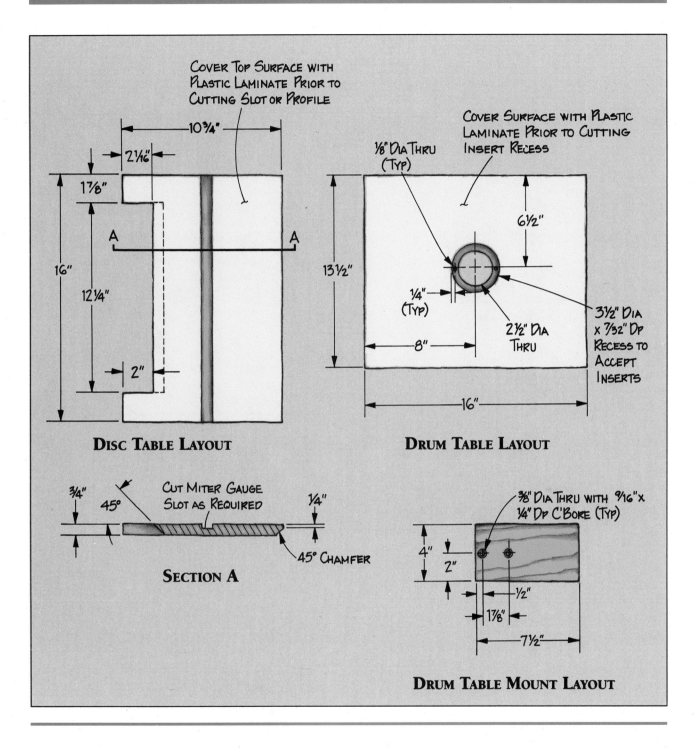

COVER TOP SURFACE WITH PLASTIC LAMINATE PRIOR TO CUTTING SLOT OR PROFILE

**DISC TABLE LAYOUT**

COVER SURFACE WITH PLASTIC LAMINATE PRIOR TO CUTTING INSERT RECESS

⅛" DIA THRU (TYP)

6½"

¼" (TYP)

2½" DIA THRU

3½" DIA x 7/32" DP RECESS TO ACCEPT INSERTS

13½"

8"

16"

**DRUM TABLE LAYOUT**

¾"

45°

CUT MITER GAUGE SLOT AS REQUIRED

¼"

45° CHAMFER

**SECTION A**

⅜" DIA THRU WITH 9/16" x ¼" DP C'BORE (TYP)

4"

2"

½"

1⅞"

7½"

**DRUM TABLE MOUNT LAYOUT**

■ the disc table mounts, as shown on the *Disc Table Mount Layout*
■ the disc table trunnions, as shown on the *Disc Table Trunnion Layout*
■ the base, as shown in the *Base Layout*

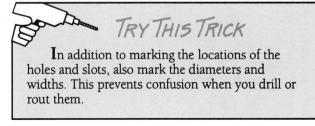

## TRY THIS TRICK

**I**n addition to marking the locations of the holes and slots, also mark the diameters and widths. This prevents confusion when you drill or rout them.

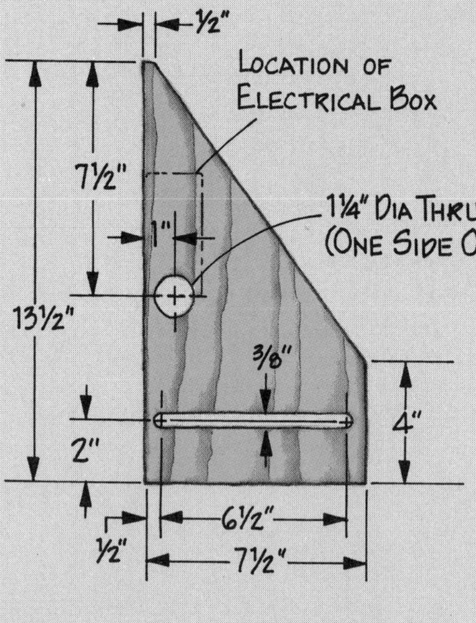
1/2"
Location of Electrical Box
7 1/2"
1"
1 1/4" Dia Thru (One Side Only)
13 1/2"
3/8"
4"
2"
1/2"
6 1/2"
7 1/2"

**Drum Table Side Layout**

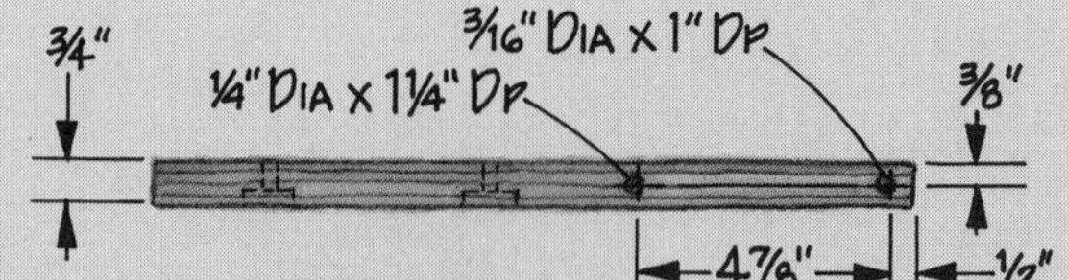
3/4"
1/4" Dia x 1 1/4" Dp
3/16" Dia x 1" Dp
3/8"
4 7/8"
1/2"

**SIDE VIEW**

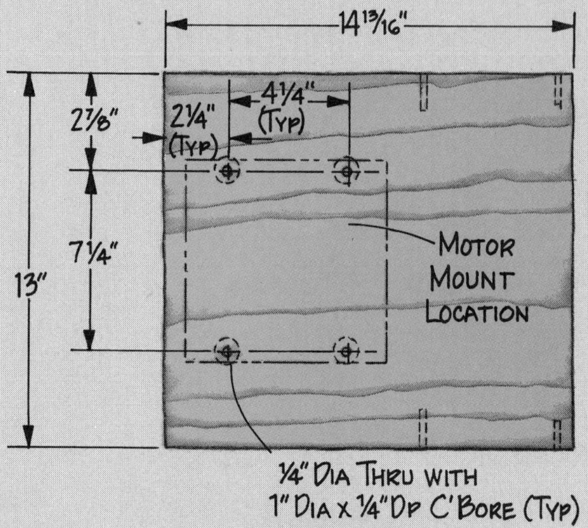
14 13/16"
2 7/8"
2 1/4" (Typ)
4 1/4" (Typ)
7 1/4"
13"
Motor Mount Location
1/4" Dia Thru with 1" Dia x 1/4" Dp C'Bore (Typ)

**TOP VIEW**

**Base Layout**

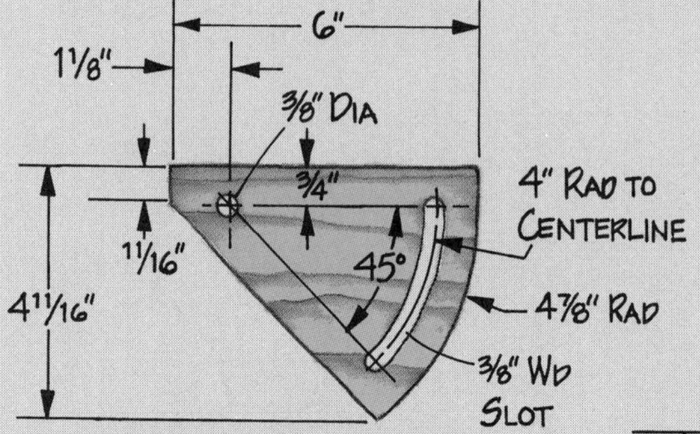
6"
1 1/8"
3/8" Dia
3/4"
11/16"
4 11/16"
4" Rad to Centerline
45°
4 7/8" Rad
3/8" Wd Slot

**Disc Table Trunnion Layout**

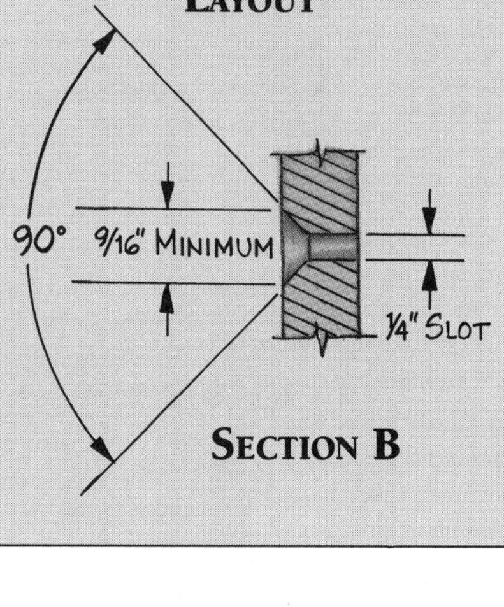
90°
9/16" Minimum
1/4" Slot

**Section B**

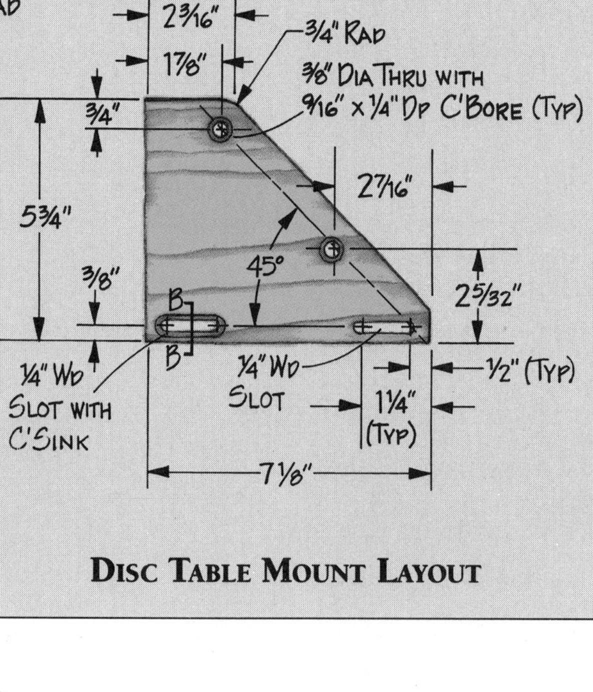
2 3/16"
1 7/8"
3/4" Rad
3/8" Dia Thru with 9/16" x 1/4" Dp C'Bore (Typ)
3/4"
2 7/16"
5 3/4"
45°
3/8"
2 5/32"
B
B
1/4" Wd Slot with C'Sink
1/4" Wd Slot
1/2" (Typ)
1 1/4" (Typ)
7 1/8"

**Disc Table Mount Layout**

**3  Drill the holes in the parts.**  Drill the holes and counterbores that you've marked in the drum table mounts, disc table mounts, disc table trunnions, and base. Also drill holes to mark the ends of the slots in the drum table sides, disc table mounts, and disc table trunnions. However, you don't yet cut any of the holes in the drum table inserts, the 1¼-inch-diameter hole in drum table side, or the 2½-inch-diameter hole in the drum table.

> **TRY THIS TRICK**
>
> **T**o drill the counterbored holes in the drum table and disc table mounts, first drill a ¹⁄₁₆-inch-diameter hole through the stacked parts to mark the locations of the holes on both sides of the stack. Drill ⁹⁄₁₆-inch-diameter, ¼-inch-deep counterbores in one face, turn the stack over, and drill them in the other face. Then drill ³⁄₈-inch-diameter holes through the stack, in the center of the counterbores.

**4  Cut the shapes of the parts.**  Using a band saw, scroll saw, or saber saw, cut the shapes of the drum table sides, drum table braces, disc table, disc table mounts, and disc table trunnions. Sand the sawed edges, then take apart all the stacked parts that you have cut and drilled, and discard the tape. *Don't cut the shape of the inserts yet; leave them stacked together.*

**5  Rout or cut the slots in the parts.**  Using straight bits and a table-mounted router, rout ³⁄₈-inch-wide slots in the drum table sides and disc table trunnions, and ¼-inch-wide slots in the disc table mounts. *(SEE FIGURE 8-1.)* You can also make these slots by cutting out the waste between the holes that mark the ends of the slots, using a coping saw, saber saw, or scroll saw.

Countersink the edges of the *inside* slots on the disc table mounts (the slots nearest the motor), as shown in *Section B*. Substitute a V-groove bit for the straight bit in the router, and cut the countersinks in the same manner that you routed the slots. If you have sawed the slots, make the countersinks with a file and rasp.

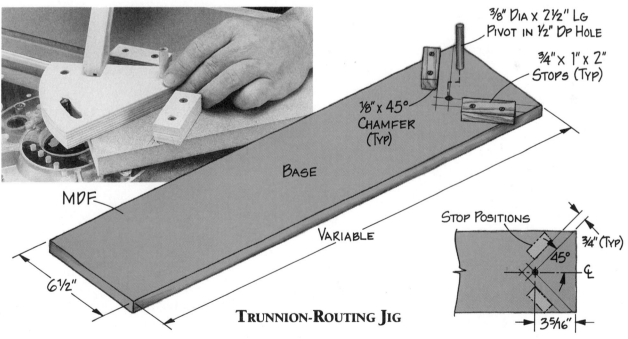

⅜" DIA X 2½" LG
PIVOT IN ½" DP HOLE

¾" X 1" X 2"
STOPS (TYP)

⅛" X 45°
CHAMFER
(TYP)

BASE

VARIABLE

MDF

6½"

**TRUNNION-ROUTING JIG**

STOP POSITIONS

¾" (TYP)

45°

Ȼ

3⁵⁄₁₆"

**STOP AND PIVOT LAYOUT**

*8-1  Use this simple jig to rout the* curved slots in the trunnions. Clamp it to a routing table so the pivot is precisely 4 inches from the axis of the bit. Fit the pivot hole in one trunnion over the pivot, and one of the holes that mark the ends of the slot over the bit. Adjust the depth of cut so the bit will cut just ¹⁄₁₆ to ⅛ inch into the trunnion. Hold the trunnion securely, turn on the router, and swing the trunnion right and left on the pivot. The stops will halt the cut when the bit reaches the ends of the slot.

Stop the router, readjust the depth of cut by raising the bit another ¹⁄₁₆ to ⅛ inch, and rout again. Repeat until you have cut the slot completely through the trunnion.

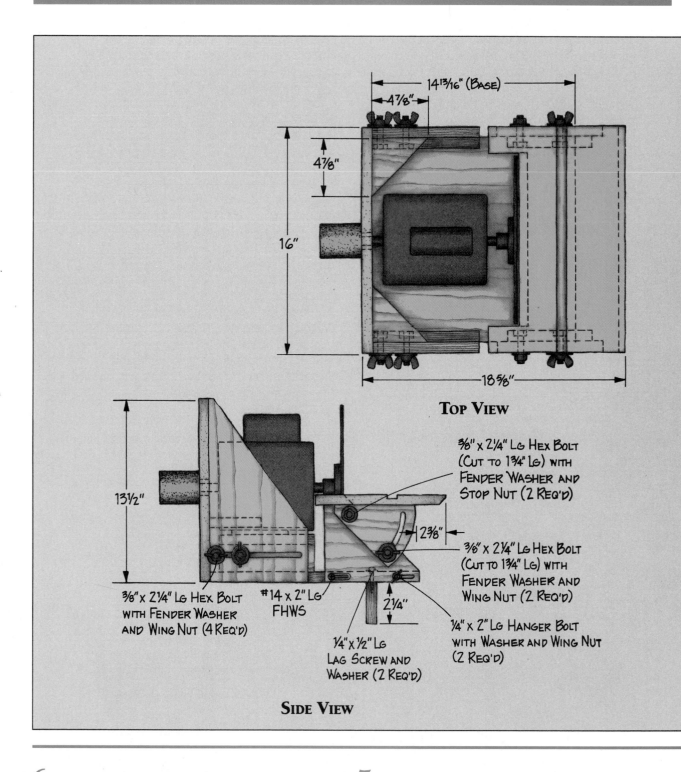

14¹³⁄₁₆" (Base)

4⁷⁄₈"

4⁷⁄₈"

16"

18⁵⁄₈"

**Top View**

13½"

2³⁄₈"

³⁄₈" x 2¼" Lg Hex Bolt
(Cut to 1¾" Lg) with
Fender Washer and
Stop Nut (2 Req'd)

³⁄₈" x 2¼" Lg Hex Bolt
(Cut to 1¾" Lg) with
Fender Washer and
Wing Nut (2 Req'd)

³⁄₈" x 2¼" Lg Hex Bolt
with Fender Washer
and Wing Nut (4 Req'd)

#14 x 2" Lg
FHWS

2¼"

¼" x ½" Lg
Lag Screw and
Washer (2 Req'd)

¼" x 2" Lg Hanger Bolt
with Washer and Wing Nut
(2 Req'd)

**Side View**

## 6  Cut a miter gauge slot in the disc table.

Measure the width and thickness of your miter gauge bar and the length of its face. From these dimensions, calculate the size and location of the miter gauge slot in the disc table. Cut this slot with a table-mounted router, or use a dado cutter.

## 7  Cut the hole and recess in the drum table.

Cut a 2½-inch-diameter hole in the drum table with a hole saw. Using a hand-held router and a rabbeting bit, cut a ½-inch-wide, ⁷⁄₃₂-inch-deep recess all around the circumference of the hole. Later, you'll make inserts to fit this recess.

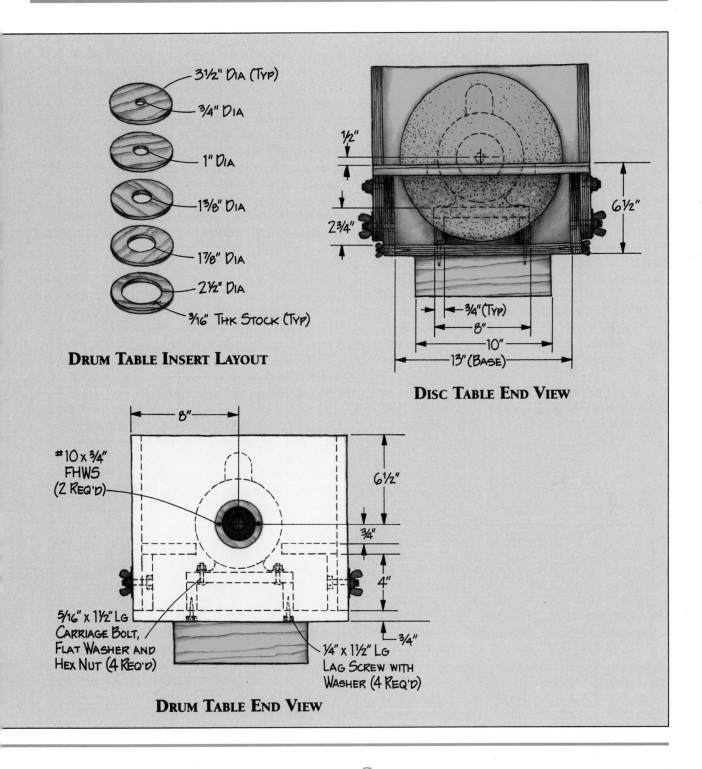

**3½" Dia (Typ)**

**¾" Dia**

**1" Dia**

**1⅜" Dia**

**1⅞" Dia**

**2½" Dia**

**³⁄₁₆" Thk Stock (Typ)**

### DRUM TABLE INSERT LAYOUT

½"

2¾"

6½"

¾" (Typ)

8"

10"

13" (Base)

### DISC TABLE END VIEW

8"

#10 x ¾"
FHWS
(2 Req'd)

6½"

¾"

4"

¾"

5/16" x 1½" Lg
Carriage Bolt,
Flat Washer and
Hex Nut (4 Req'd)

¼" x 1½" Lg
Lag Screw with
Washer (4 Req'd)

### DRUM TABLE END VIEW

**Note:** Measure the thickness of the insert stock before you cut the recess. *Most* ¼-inch plywood is ⁷⁄₃₂ inch thick, but not all. If the stock is thinner or thicker, change the depth of the recess to compensate.

**8  Drill the hole in the drum table side.**  Drill a 1¼-inch-diameter access hole in *one* of the drum table sides. This hole will be used to run wires between the switch box and the motor.

**9** **Assemble the base and mounts.** Lightly sand all the parts you have made so far. Attach the motor base to the motor mounts and the drum table mounts to the base with glue and utility screws. Attach the motor mount assembly to the base with lag screws, driving them up from the bottom of the base.

Install the hanger bolts in the *outside holes* (those nearest the end) in the edges of the base. Put the outside slots in the disc table mounts over the hanger bolts and secure them with fender washers and wing nuts. Install #14 flathead wood screws in the *inside* holes and slots.

**10** **Fasten a clamp bar to the base.** If you intend to clamp this tool to your workbench when you use it, fasten a clamp bar to the bottom of the base with lag screws. To secure the disc-and-drum sander to the bench, just clamp the bar in your vise. The position of the clamping bar will depend on where you have the vise mounted on your workbench and how you want to orient the sander when you use it.

**11** **Assemble the drum and disc tables.** Cut the 2¼-inch-long hex bolts to 1⅞ inches long, using a hacksaw. Fasten the drum table sides to their mounts with hex bolts, fender washers, and wing nuts. Fasten the disc table trunnions to their mounts with hex bolts, fender washers, wing nuts, and stop nuts. (Use the stop nuts for the bolts on which the trunnions pivot.) Tighten all the nuts enough to draw the heads of the hex bolts into the counterbores.

Loosen the nuts and adjust the sides so the outside edges are flush with the base. Adjust the trunnions so they are horizontal, then tighten all the nuts again. Fasten the drum table to its sides and the disc table to its trunnions with glue and utility screws. Also attach the drum table braces to the drum table assembly with glue and screws.

After the glue dries, loosen the wing nuts. Check that both tables slide in and out and that the disc sander table tilts easily. If the action is difficult, or the tables bind, you may have to file the inside edges of the slots or adjust the tightness of the stop nuts and #14 screws.

**12** **Attach the motor to its base.** Mount the sanding drum to one motor shaft and the sanding disc to the other. Place the motor on the motor mount assembly and center the sanding drum in the hole in the drum table. Check that the sanding disc is parallel to the inside edge of the disc table. Mark the position

of the slots or holes in the motor's base on the mounting assembly. Remove the motor and drill ⁵⁄₁₆-inch-diameter holes in the wooden mount to match those in the motor. Fasten the motor to its mount with carriage bolts, washers, and hex nuts.

**13** **Attach the switch box and wire the motor.** Open up a hole in the end of the switch box and another in the side. Secure a right-angle cord clamp to the end of the box, and a straight cord clamp to the side. Fasten the other straight cord clamp to the motor. Position the box on the drum table side with the 1¼-inch-diameter hole so the right-angle clamp goes through the hole. Secure the box to the side with panhead screws.

Drill holes in the box cover for the switches and mount them in the cover. Install a power cord in the box's straight cord clamp, with sufficient leads to attach it to a switch. Following the *Wiring Diagram*, attach the cord to the double-pole, single-throw switch, ground it to the box, and run wires between the switches and the motor. Double-check your connections, then attach the cover to the box.

The single-throw switch turns the motor on and off, while the double-throw switch reverses the direction of rotation. Being able to reverse the motor is not absolutely necessary, but it increases the versatility of the tool and helps keep the abrasives cleaner. By changing the rotation of the disc and drum now and then, you prevent the resins and sawdust from becoming impacted on the abrasives. This, in turn, helps the abrasives last longer.

---

### A SAFETY REMINDER

**I**f you turn on the sander for the first time and it doesn't rotate but just sits there and hums, turn it off *immediately*. You've wired the motor incorrectly. This won't hurt the motor as long as you don't leave it on for more than a few seconds. Shut the sander off quickly, unplug it, and recheck your connections. If you have trouble with the wiring, or feel uncomfortable with the task, have someone with more experience do it for you. Any licensed electrician or motor repair shop will be able to help.

---

**Note:** Don't turn the sander on with the reversing switch in the *center* position, if you have purchased a center-off double-throw switch. The motor won't start, and it may be harmed if you leave the switch on for more than a few seconds.

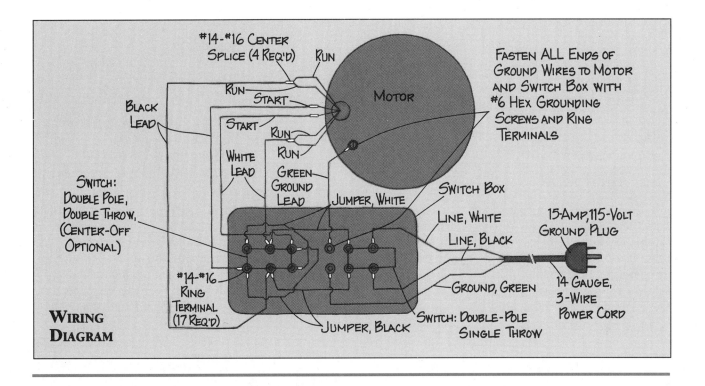

#14-#16 Center Splice (4 Req'd)
Run
Motor
Fasten All Ends of Ground Wires to Motor and Switch Box with #6 Hex Grounding Screws and Ring Terminals

Run
Start
Start
Run
Run
Green Ground Lead
White Lead
Black Lead

Switch: Double Pole, Double Throw, (Center-Off Optional)

Jumper, White
Switch Box
Line, White
Line, Black

15-Amp, 115-Volt Ground Plug

#14-#16 Ring Terminal (17 Req'd)

Ground, Green

14 Gauge, 3-Wire Power Cord

Jumper, Black
Switch: Double-Pole Single Throw

**WIRING DIAGRAM**

**14 Grind the bevel on the disc table.** The inside edge of the disc table (closest to the disc) must be beveled at 45 degrees. This allows you to position the table close to the sanding disc when the table is tilted. To make this bevel, affix coarse (50-grit) abrasive to the disc. Tilt the table to 45 degrees and pull it away from the disc. Tighten the wing nuts that secure the trunnions, but leave those nuts loose that secure the disc table mounts. Turn on the sander and slowly push the table toward the disc until you have ground the bevel.

**15 Make the inserts.** Use a band saw, scroll saw, or saber saw to cut the outside diameter of the stacked inserts, running the blade just a little wide of the line. Adjust the disc table square to the disc and sand up to the line. Check the fit of the bottom and top inserts in the drum table. If they're too tight, sand the edges until the fit is perfect.

Drill 3/16-inch-diameter holes through the stack, 1/4 inch from the circumference, as shown in the *Drum Table Insert Layout*. Take the stack apart and discard the tape. Countersink all the 3/16-inch-diameter holes, then cut holes of various sizes through the centers of the inserts.

Place one insert in the drum table and mark the positions of the countersunk holes on the recess. Remove the insert and drill 1/8-inch-diameter pilot holes at the

marks. Secure the insert in the recess with #10 flathead wood screws.

**16 Finish the disc-and-drum sander.** Remove the motor, switch box, and power cord from the sander. Then detach the drum table, insert, disc table, and disc table sides. Set all the hardware aside and finish the wooden surfaces with several coats of tung oil. When the finish dries, rub it out with paste wax and buff thoroughly — wax will help the moving parts slide smoothly. Finally, reassemble the sander and replace the motor.

## TIPS FOR USING THE DISC-AND-DRUM SANDER

■ To use small, shaft-mounted sanding drums, purchase a drill chuck that fits the motor arbor. Remove the large drum, replace it with the chuck, and mount the smaller drums in the chuck.

■ Use the inserts to reduce the diameter of the opening around the sanding drum. Keep the opening as small as possible. Not only does this provide more support for the workpiece, it reduces the pinch point and makes the tool safer to use.

■ Whenever you change the tilt of the disc table, readjust the horizontal position to keep the table as close as possible to the disc. This, too, provides more support and reduces the pinch point.

# 9

# SANDPAPER DISPENSER

One of the most economical and efficient ways to buy sandpaper is in 4½-inch-wide rolls. Tear off specific lengths for quarter-sheet sanders, half-sheet sanders, sanding blocks, and special applications as you need them. This is easier than marking, folding, and tearing standard sandpaper sheets, and you won't have a lot of partial sheets left over when the job is done.

There are several commercial dispensers available for sandpaper rolls, but this shop-made dispenser offers a useful advantage over them. Lines on the top and back automatically *measure* the length of the paper before you cut it. Simply pull the sandpaper out to the proper line, swing the cutter bar in place, and cut the paper. You get the right length every time, with no waste.

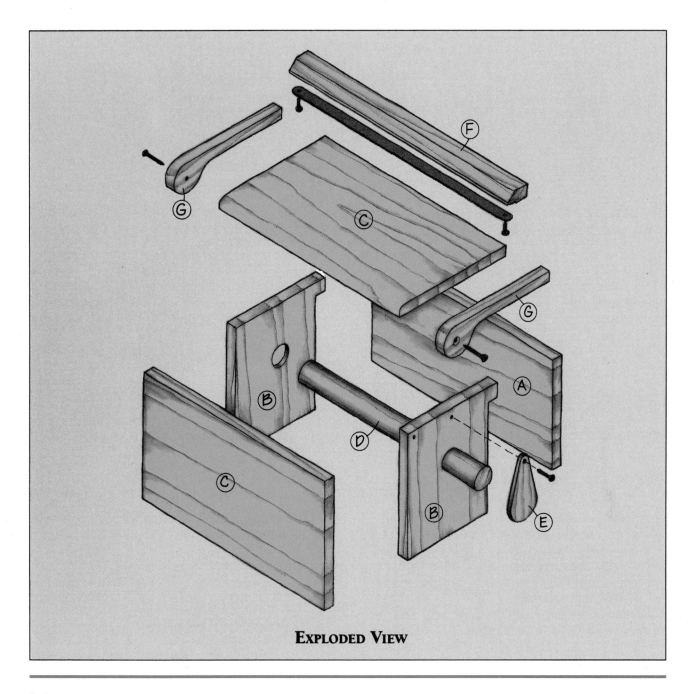

**EXPLODED VIEW**

# MATERIALS LIST (FINISHED DIMENSIONS)

## Parts

A. Front        $\frac{1}{2}$″ x 5$\frac{1}{4}$″ x 10$\frac{1}{4}$″
B. Sides (2)        $\frac{1}{2}$″ x 4$\frac{1}{2}$″ x 6″
C. Back/top (2)    $\frac{1}{2}$″ x 6″ x 10$\frac{1}{4}$″
D. Rod            1″ dia. x 10″
E. Keeper        $\frac{1}{4}$″ x 1$\frac{1}{2}$″ x 2$\frac{3}{4}$″
F. Cutter bar      $\frac{1}{2}$″ x 1″ x 12$\frac{1}{2}$″
G. Arms (2)        $\frac{1}{2}$″ x 1$\frac{1}{2}$″ x 6″

## Hardware

#6 x 1″ Flathead wood screws (2)
#6 x $\frac{3}{4}$″ Flathead wood screw
#6 x $\frac{1}{2}$″ Panhead wood screws (2)
12″ Hacksaw blade

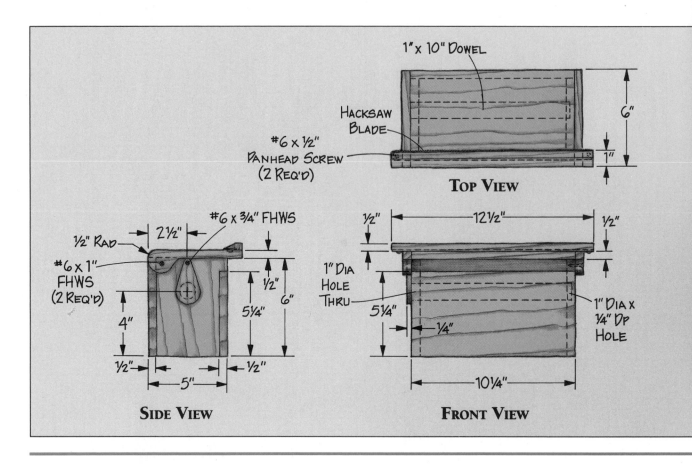

# PLAN OF PROCEDURE

**1 Select the stock and cut the parts to size.**
To make this project, you need about 2 board feet of 4/4 (four-quarters) stock. Select a hard but inexpensive wood such as ash, birch, or poplar, or hardwood left over from another project. The dispenser shown was made from scrap maple.

Plane the wood to ½ inch thick, then cut the parts to the sizes specified in the Materials List, except for the keeper. Plane a small amount of ½-inch-thick stock to ¼ inch to make this part; or, if you have a scrap of ¼-inch-thick stock lying about, use that.

**Note:** As shown, this dispenser will hold two 4½-inch-wide sandpaper rolls. This capacity was determined by the length of a standard hacksaw blade — 12 inches. If you wish to dispense more than two rolls, either make additional dispensers or make a longer dispenser using a ½-inch-wide band saw blade instead of a hacksaw blade.

**2 Lay out the parts.** The sides and the arms are duplicates of one another. To save time, stack the parts face to face before you machine them, using double-faced carpet tape to stick them together. Lay out the shape of the arms and the location of the hole, as shown in the *Arm Layout,* on just one piece in the stack. Also lay out the sides, as shown in the *Side View,* and the keeper, as shown in the *Keeper Layout.*

**3 Drill the holes in the parts.** Drill a 1-inch-diameter hole through one side and ¼ inch deep into the second. Also drill and countersink ⅛-inch-diameter holes in the arms and the keeper.

**4 Cut the shapes of the parts.** Using a band saw or a scroll saw, cut the shapes of the sides, arms, and keeper. Also cut a 45-degree chamfer in the top edge of the cutter bar, and a ⅜-inch-wide, 1⁄16-inch-deep rabbet in the bottom edge, as shown in the *Cutter Bar Profile.* With a table-mounted router and a ½-inch quarter-round bit, round over the back edge of the top, as shown in the *Side View.* Sand or file the sawed and routed edges, then take the stacks apart and discard the tape.

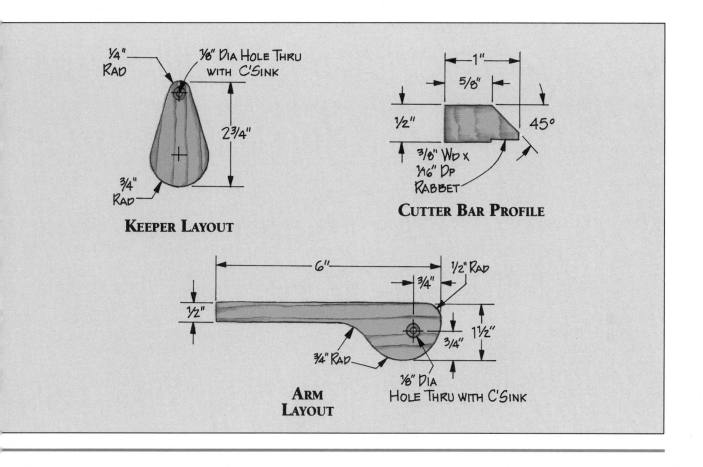

**KEEPER LAYOUT**

**CUTTER BAR PROFILE**

**ARM LAYOUT**

**5  Assemble the dispenser.**  Sand the parts of the dispenser, then glue the front, back, top, and sides together. Let the glue dry, and sand the glue joints flush and clean.

Slide the rod into the 1-inch-diameter holes in the sides. Fasten the keeper over the through hole, using a ³/₄-inch-long flathead screw. Tighten the screw so it's snug, but not so tight that the keeper won't pivot.

Fasten the arms to the sides with 1-inch-long flathead wood screws, leaving the screws a little loose so the arms swing easily. Also attach the hacksaw blade to the cutter bar with ¹/₂-inch-long panhead screws. Glue the cutter bar to the arms so the front edge of the bar is flush with the front ends of the arms, as shown in the *Top View*.

**6  Finish the dispenser.**  Detach the hacksaw blade from the cutter bar. Also remove the cutter bar and arms assembly and the keeper from the dispenser housing. Set the metal hardware aside, and do any necessary touch-up sanding on the wooden parts. Finish the dispenser with two coats of tung oil, and

rub it out with steel wool and paste wax. Buff the wax and reassemble the parts.

## TIPS FOR USING THE SANDPAPER DISPENSER

■ To load the dispenser, swing the keeper up and remove the rod. Place one or two sandpaper rolls inside the housing so the cutter bar will contact the uncoated side, and insert the rod through them. Swing the keeper back down over the end of the rod.

■ Determine the lengths of the sandpaper sheets that you use. Measure from the edge of the hacksaw blade along the top and down the back, and make marks for the lengths needed. Scribe lines across the top and back at the marks.

■ To cut the sandpaper to length, first swing the cutter bar back. Pull the paper out of the housing, across the top, and — if necessary — down the back, until the paper's edge is flush with the proper mark. Swing the cutter bar in place over the paper (again, it should contact the *uncoated* side), then tear the paper along the hacksaw blade.

# INDEX

Note: Page references in *italic* indicate photographs or illustrations.
**Boldface** references indicate charts or tables.

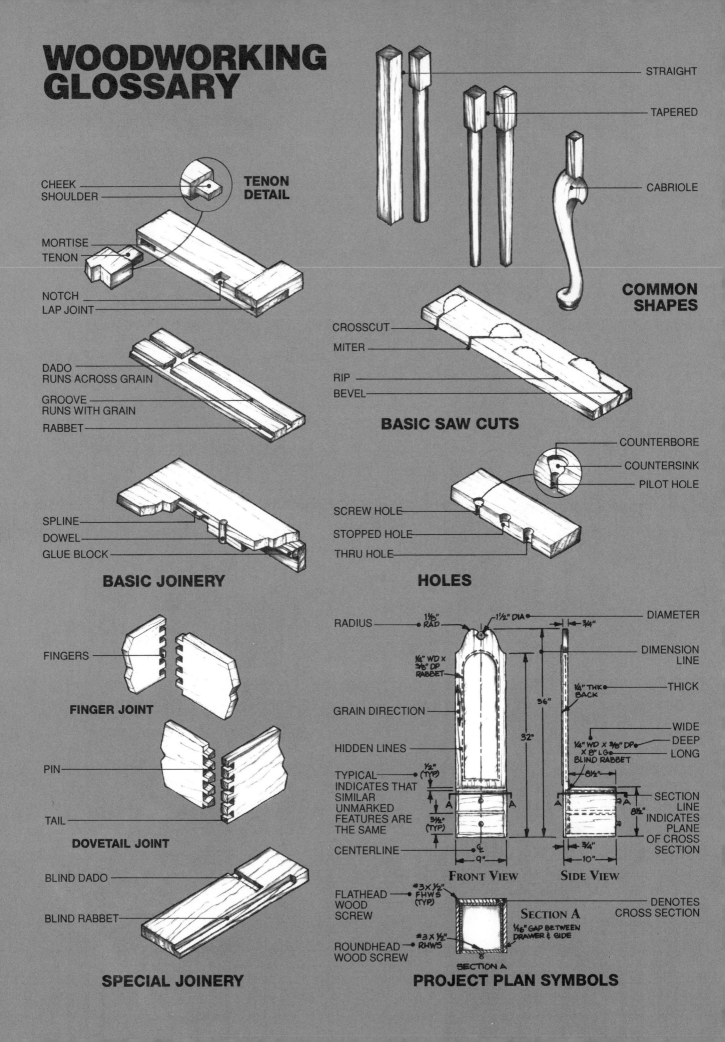

# WOODWORKING GLOSSARY

## TENON DETAIL
CHEEK
SHOULDER

MORTISE
TENON
NOTCH
LAP JOINT

## BASIC JOINERY
DADO RUNS ACROSS GRAIN
GROOVE RUNS WITH GRAIN
RABBET
SPLINE
DOWEL
GLUE BLOCK

## FINGER JOINT
FINGERS

## DOVETAIL JOINT
PIN
TAIL

## SPECIAL JOINERY
BLIND DADO
BLIND RABBET

## COMMON SHAPES
STRAIGHT
TAPERED
CABRIOLE

## BASIC SAW CUTS
CROSSCUT
MITER
RIP
BEVEL

## HOLES
COUNTERBORE
COUNTERSINK
PILOT HOLE
SCREW HOLE
STOPPED HOLE
THRU HOLE

## PROJECT PLAN SYMBOLS
RADIUS
1⅛" RAD
1½" DIA
¾"
DIAMETER
DIMENSION LINE
¼" WD x ⅜" DP RABBET
¼" THK BACK
THICK
36"
32"
GRAIN DIRECTION
¼" WD x ⅜" DP X 8" LG BLIND RABBET
WIDE
DEEP
LONG
8½"
HIDDEN LINES
TYPICAL INDICATES THAT SIMILAR UNMARKED FEATURES ARE THE SAME
½" (TYP)
A
A
A
A
SECTION LINE INDICATES PLANE OF CROSS SECTION
8½"
3½" (TYP)
CENTERLINE
¾"
¢
9"
10"
FRONT VIEW
SIDE VIEW
FLATHEAD WOOD SCREW
#3 x ½" FHWS (TYP)
SECTION A
DENOTES CROSS SECTION
1/16" GAP BETWEEN DRAWER & SIDE
ROUNDHEAD WOOD SCREW
#3 x ½" RHWS
SECTION A